Profiles in ACHIEVEMENT

CT
120
H65
1987

Profiles in ACHIEVEMENT

CHARLES M. HOLLOWAY

COLLEGE ENTRANCE EXAMINATION BOARD, NEW YORK

METROPOLITAN COLLEGE
OF NEW YORK LIBRARY
75 Varick Street 12th Fl.
New York, NY 10013

In all of its book publishing activities the College Board endeavors to present the works of authors who are well qualified to write with authority on the subject at hand, and to present accurate and timely information. However, the opinions, interpretations, and conclusions of the authors are their own and do not necessarily represent those of the College Board; nothing contained herein should be assumed to represent an official position of the College Board, or any of its members.

Copies of this book are available from your local bookseller or may be ordered from College Board Publications, Box 886, New York, New York 10101. The price is $15.95. Editorial inquiries concerning this book should be directed to Editorial Office, The College Board, 45 Columbus Avenue, New York, New York 10023-6992.

Copyright © 1987 by Charles M. Holloway. All rights reserved. Printed in the United States of America.

Cover design by Terrence Fehr. Photo credits: Arthur Ashe, Jr., p. 2, courtesy of ProServ; Anthony Kahn, p. 60, courtesy of Joseph Kennedy; Suzanne Saunders, p. 102, courtesy of *American Bar Association Journal*.

The College Board, Scholastic Aptitude Test, SAT, and the acorn logo are registered trademarks of the College Entrance Examination Board.

ISBN: 0-87447-291-1
Library of Congress Catalog Number: 87-072158

9 8 7 6 5 4 3 2 1

Contents

Introduction   vii

1
ARTHUR ASHE, JR.   3

2
HENRY CISNEROS   21

3
KAREN HALL   41

4
ANTHONY KAHN   61

5
WINSTON HONG LIEU 85

6
SUZANNE SAUNDERS 103

7
SYBIL JORDAN STEVENSON 123

8
CAROLYN THOMPSON 145

Index 167

Introduction

These are stories about how eight successful men and women have used hard work, determination, self-esteem, and a keen respect for education to reach their separate goals. They overcame barriers of race, gender, tradition, and economic circumstance. Some of their victories are bittersweet, involving personal sacrifice, but all testify to the rewards of an unswerving commitment to excellence.

Each of the individuals described here learned how to combine intelligence with true grit, how to win against great odds, and how to use a unique talent to advantage. Most of them worked their way through high school or college or both. It didn't seem to hurt them, and probably increased their appreciation for both education and work.

Almost all of them have broken new ground in their jobs and professions. Consider Arthur Ashe in sports, whacking tennis balls on the rough asphalt courts in Richmond—a skinny, undersized boy with less-than-perfect eyesight, who practiced harder and longer than anyone else to become the best tennis player in the country, black or white.

Or take Suzanne Saunders in the field of law, who at age 15 was married and pregnant, a potential high school dropout. But she didn't leave school; she found her own strengths, returned after the birth of her child to graduate with her class, and then worked her way through college and law school.

Or Winston Hong Lieu, a teenage Vietnamese refugee,

INTRODUCTION

who rode a leaky boat to freedom, carrying with him only an English-language dictionary and a burning desire to excel.

Or Sybil Jordan Stevenson, walking bravely up the steps of Little Rock's Central High School between lines of soldiers, breaking down 100 years of segregation, and later going on to a top corporate job.

As I traveled more than 25,000 miles around the United States visiting the homes, schools, and businesses of these people, I learned that there was no single magic formula for their successes, but I did gain valuable insights into their motivation and persistence, and I picked up some important clues about how they made the system work for them.

These are, as the title suggests, essentially *profiles*—concise accounts of dramatic and sometimes controversial lives marked by strong, supportive families, creative and understanding teachers, and, especially, pride.

From Ashe's business headquarters high above Manhattan to the handsome marble corridors of the Oklahoma capitol where state representative Carolyn Thompson spends her working days and on to Tony Kahn's one-room hogan on the high plains of Arizona, I was cordially welcomed by the parents, teachers, and colleagues who helped shape the lives of these remarkable leaders.

Throughout the interviews, I felt the strong bonds of kinship and loyalty that had begun early and lasted a long time—through school and college and beyond. Talking with Ashe revived my memories of him winning the U.S. tennis championship at Forest Hills and standing proudly next to his father as they lifted the trophy high, together.

The research and travel had other bonuses, too. There were memorable meals along the way, interludes that conveyed a sense of personality and place. There was spicy mulligatawny soup and mango ice cream with Karen Hall in the Twentieth Century Fox commissary, where writers and stars from *Moonlighting* mingled at lunch with the grips, gaffers, and producers of TV shows and films.

INTRODUCTION

More than once, I was treated to "Mom's" specialties, like the cool and ethereal lime chiffon pie that Elvira Cisneros served me on a steamy night in San Antonio. Or the succulent barbecued ribs and sweet potato pie that Lorraine Jordan fixed for me in Little Rock while we talked about her daughter's ordeal at Central High.

Simply put, these are inspiring stories that offer hope in troubled times. Each carries a special sense of renewal, and together they demonstrate once again the vast opportunities that still exist in our country for those prepared to seize them.

Profiles in
ACHIEVEMENT

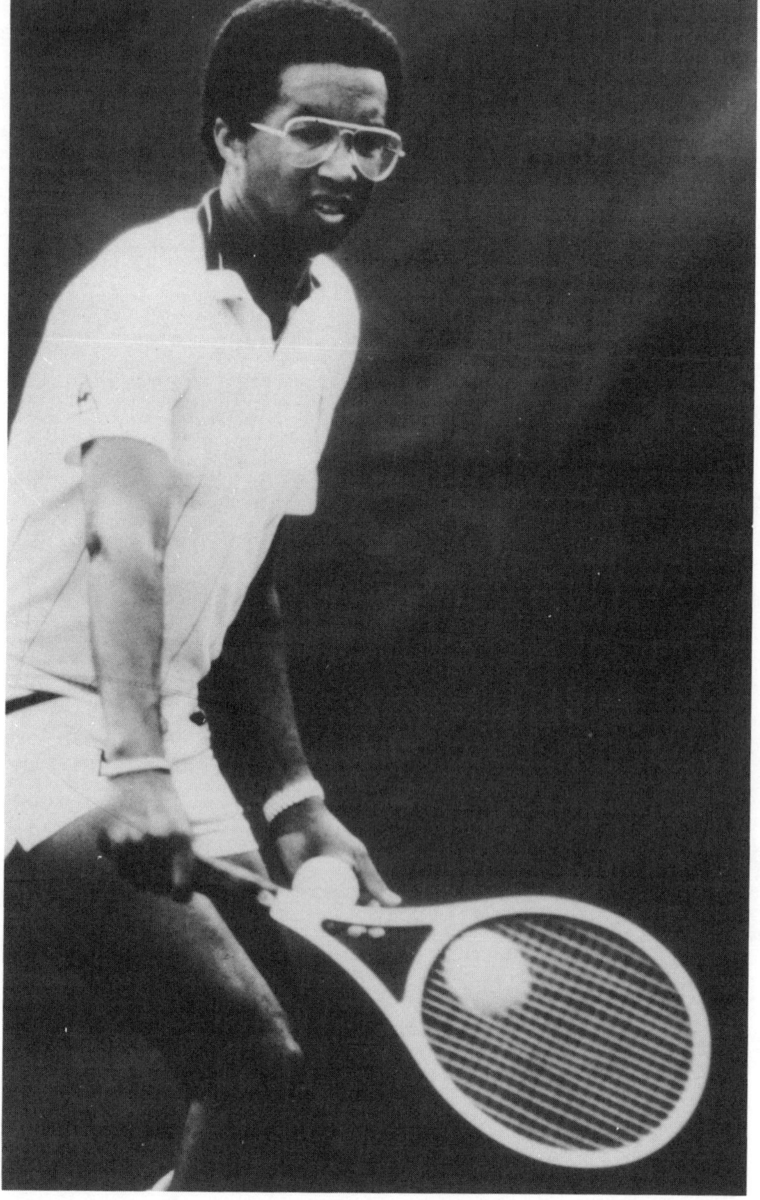

Chapter 1

ARTHUR ASHE, JR.

Arthur Ashe, Jr., was in a relaxed mood on a winter day in early 1986, sitting in a blue-gray velour chair in the seventeenth-floor conference room of the ProServ corporation, overlooking the midday traffic on Lexington Avenue in Manhattan. At 6'1", 160 pounds, he looked as lean and fit as he did more than a decade ago when he was winning the U.S. Open Tennis championship, Wimbledon, and other tournaments. He was wearing tan slacks and a dark blue sports shirt with white pin stripes over a blue turtleneck. He looked fresh and energetic despite a hectic schedule of writing, television appearances, and worldwide travel in connection with ProServ, ABC-TV Sports, and other enterprises. He was thinking about the landmark series of books on black athletes in America *(A Hard Road to Glory)* that he had been working on and reminding himself of plans for celebrating the anniversary of his wedding to Jeanne Moutoussamy coming up in late February. In the midst of all of his commitments, he was also looking forward to another personal event, sched-

CHAPTER ONE

uled in Richmond later in the year—the twenty-fifth reunion of a special group from the 1961 graduating class at Maggie Walker High School.

The threads of sports and schooling have been interwoven throughout Ashe's life; both helped sustain him as he grew up during some of the most turbulent years in recent American history. Now in his mid forties, he has somewhat the look of a scholar—which he is—but he seems comfortable in his latest role of sports executive. His business activities mesh well with other facets of his personal and social interests. Tennis remains central to his life—it has been since the spring day more than 30 years ago when he walked onto the asphalt surface of the public playground at Brook Field in Richmond, Virginia, to take his first tennis lesson with the local college star, Ron Charity.

Ashe's career as a pioneering black player in an all-white sport spanned a quarter of a century of major change in sports, education, and the social fabric of the country. He was born on July 10, 1943, in St. Phillips, a segregated hospital in Richmond, 4 years before blacks could play baseball in the major leagues, 5 years before President Harry Truman ordered the desegregation of the armed forces, and a full 10 years before the U.S. Supreme Court (in *Brown* v. *Board of Education*) struck a vital legal blow in the fight to open up public education. He learned tennis on a black playground supervised by his father; he graduated from black elementary and high schools; and only when he entered college at the University of California at Los Angeles and served as an army officer did he begin to transcend the formidable and sensitive barriers that had governed his life and the lives of so many of his generation. Sports, education, and military service all helped open vital doors of opportunity to Ashe, but he remembers, too, with fondness and emotion, that it was the strength, courage, and loyalty of his father that provided the essential foundations and guided and motivated him through his formative years.

ARTHUR ASHE, JR.

"He never went beyond the sixth grade himself," Ashe recalled, "but he helped push me along, broaden my horizons, develop a sense of myself.

"I wasn't very old ... maybe six or seven ... when he bought us the *World Book Encyclopedia*. I mean, the real *World Book*, not the junior edition ... I used to spend hours just opening up the volumes and reading subjects at random.... I think my father still has the books, somewhere."

Ashe's mother had taught him to read at about age four, only three years before she died, and by the time he entered first grade, his father knew Arthur would become the best reader at the Baker Elementary School. He did. While he was still in grade school, Arthur got a job collecting bottles and newspapers. A fringe benefit of that job was being allowed to keep some of the discarded copies of *National Geographic*, which he read avidly and which stimulated his interest in other nations and peoples. He later became a life member of the National Geographic Society and the influence of this ongoing pursuit is reflected in his travels around the world.

Today, after recovering from a heart attack and major heart surgery that curtailed his tennis-playing career in 1979, Ashe maintains a carefully modulated but extremely demanding schedule of business and social activities from a base in New York City. He has retired from his job as captain of the U.S. Davis Cup team though he is still active in the program, and also remains closely involved with tennis through his work as resident professional at the Doral Country Club in Miami and as color commentator for ABC-TV Sports. He is a vice-president of marketing of Le Coq Sportif tennis clothes (worn by Yannick Noah, among others) and promotes sales worldwide for his own tennis racquets, made by Head.

During a conversation that took place in an informal conference room decorated with bright LeRoy Neiman paintings of a McEnroe–Lendl tennis match, Ashe talked about a recently completed TV documentary on black athletes that

CHAPTER ONE

he narrated and helped develop. The show was an outgrowth of the series of books he had spent nearly three years researching and writing. "It almost became an obsession with me," he said. "No one had ever done a comprehensive and complete history of the black athlete in America before." His interest in black history derives in part from a deep pride and thorough knowledge of his own family roots, which date to 1735 when the slave ship H.M.S. *Doddington* brought his forbears to tidewater Virginia. His love of writing and language grew out of his early reading and the continued encouragement of both his parents and teachers.

Ashe did well in school from the beginning, and some of his warmest memories center around the early days when he started high school at Maggie Walker and encountered the unique group of students and friends who made up the twenty-fifth reunion group.

Maggie Walker High School was built in 1947 and named after Richmond's first black woman bank president. Today it is a weathered but well-maintained red-brick building at Lombardy and Leigh streets, only a couple of hundred yards south of where Interstate 64 cuts a swath through town. The two-story school sits in an industrial area bounded by shabby wooden row houses, factories, an auto-body shop, fast-food joints, an elevated highway, and grassy playing fields. Inside the main entry stands the school's athletic trophy cases documenting victories of the Dragons in football, baseball, and track. There was no tennis team in Ashe's day, and there isn't one now. The present school houses about 700 students from grades 6 through 10, and students go on to Marshall School for their last two years.

The yearbooks from Ashe's time suggest that most graduates did not aspire to academic or professional careers; most seniors planned on vocational training to become beauticians, lab technicians, clerks, shoe repairmen, bricklayers, and mechanics. A small number said they wanted careers in teaching, engineering, and social work. Reflecting perhaps the influence of the 1957 Soviet sputnik, the faculty at Maggie Walker included a Russian-language teacher, Mr. Yurcenko.

Ashe and a handful of able students were singled out by the principal, J. Harry Williams, to go into a special class when they arrived at Maggie Walker from their junior high school.

"Now, when I look back," Ashe said, "I realize that Mr. Williams had set up his own sort of tracking system. He had identified some bright youngsters from Benjamin Graves Junior High School and put them together in a special class . . . our home room teacher was Marvin Powell . . . I guess there were about 32 of us. The instructions given to our teachers were to 'take them as far as you can take them. Forget the standard curriculum.'

"We had some great teachers," Ashe continued. "There was Mr. Powell, of course, who also taught biology. And Miss Ransom in geometry, and Miss Austin for algebra. They helped us all, inspired us to do our best. They made academic work exciting . . . something to be proud of.

"It's interesting, by the way," Ashe noted, "that most of my friends in this group had little to do with athletics. They have all gone on to excel in other things. My best friend, Ralph Williams, is now a tenor; Pamela Wood Fraley is a soprano who sings in Boston; and Isaiah Jackson became a conductor." Another close friend, Joey Kennedy, whose father taught music at Maggie Walker, became a jazz musician and earned a master's degree in music. Others are now scientists, college professors, and writers. "We all knew we were talented," Ashe said, "but we knew our talents wouldn't be appreciated in Richmond, so we left." He pointed out with more than a little irony that these able young people, the brains and leaders of the class of '61, all felt compelled to leave Richmond to pursue their careers and professions. But now, more than 25 years later, he observed, "some are going back. Things are still changing."

Walking around the comfortably furnished conference

CHAPTER ONE

room high above Lexington Avenue, Ashe thought back to his childhood experiences, times he once defined as "a series of concentric circles—the house on Sledd Street at the center, with the next circle Brook Field, and finally the city of Richmond—each circle was largely defined by black people ... but at each level I was nurtured, loved, and challenged to develop my potential to its full capacity.... My first 17 years set the stage for the way I view the world. I grew up as an underdog."

Certainly, his teachers at Maggie Walker were important and played a vital role in helping him make key transitions in his early life, but there were some other strong and supportive people, mostly men closely associated with tennis, who shaped his future.

The first was Ron Charity, a slim, graceful college student at Virginia Union, who was one of the top black tennis players in the country and practiced regularly at Brook Field. He gave the seven-year-old Arthur his first lessons and made him aware of the barriers faced by blacks in sports at that time. As late as the 1960s, blacks could not play most sports (particularly tennis) on a mixed basis in the south.

Despite Ashe's small size and slender physique, he had, even in the early days, an unusual stamina and a wiry strength that helped him become an excellent baseball player as well as tennis champion. When he walked onto the asphalt court in 1950 for the first of endless practice sessions with Charity throughout the spring and summer, Ashe had little idea that this 78-by-36-foot rectangle, precisely marked by faded white lines defining the service areas and back court, would become the focus of his world outside home and school for many years to come. The basic space would not change, but the variations in surroundings and surfaces would be almost infinite as the years passed, his skills improved, and he progressed from a brilliant amateur player to a world-class professional tennis star. First, there were the clay courts in Lynchburg; then the public hard courts in other cities;

the carefully groomed college facilities at UCLA and at Princeton; the clipped grass at Forest Hills and Wimbledon; the synthetic turf of indoor arenas; and the rough pavements of Manhattan, where he once played an exhibition match with the net strung across a city street.

While sharpening his basic skills with Ron Charity, Ashe also developed the determined, competitive, and self-contained nature—the cool assurance—that came to characterize his career in tennis and business.

One of the first extensions of Ashe's world came when he was 10 and Charity recommended him to Dr. Robert Johnson, a prominent physician from Lynchburg, Virginia, who encouraged and helped young black players in the area. Johnson was impressed with the boy and invited him to live at the Johnson home for two weeks in the summer of 1953 to practice and learn on Johnson's private tennis court, to become both protégé and apprentice. Ashe joined other talented players who were involved in Johnson's tennis enterprise in regular and intensive practice sessions, and eventually went on trips with them to play in tournaments as far away as Washington, D.C. Ashe considers Dr. Johnson a major influence on his life, perhaps second only to his father in developing attitudes, perceptions, and a realistic approach to the many challenges that would face him on and off the tennis court.

"He simply would not accept any kids who could not carry out his standards," Ashe remembered. "He taught us tennis, and more, he taught us a whole way of life." Ashe once remarked that Johnson had taught his pupils the strictest of manners, "an unshakable Oriental calm."

"We were not instructed to be sportsmen, but to be downright benefactors, to give any reasonably close decision to an opponent."

Robert Johnson had himself been an outstanding athlete in college and an all-American football player while attending Lincoln University in Pennsylvania. As an active player

CHAPTER ONE

and coach in black tennis circles in the 1950s, he was familiar with the segregated conditions of U.S. tennis, but groomed Ashe and others for a time when they might be able to compete with white players. Sometimes on trips to tournaments, the young players were faced with the painful realities of segregation—eating packed lunches of fried chicken and homemade potato salad in Dr. Johnson's Buick because they were barred from restaurants. "But," Ashe recalled, "it was no big deal, and if you had traveled around a bit, you knew what to expect. You did hear, though, that above Washington, D.C., it was not that way."

All the lessons stuck with Arthur Ashe during his long career playing against blacks and whites, on private and public courts, competing in Europe, Australia, and Africa. He came to be known widely as a sportsman and a gentleman, neither of which detracted from his fierce competitive nature.

On the tennis court in Lynchburg and the playing fields in Richmond, Ashe developed an unswerving commitment to quality and fairness that came to play a part in the changes that brought steadily increasing numbers of black athletes into college and professional sports. Thousands of young blacks, for generations denied the opportunity to participate, or even to enter higher education in many states, were sought, recruited, and enrolled in colleges and universities that had never seen a black face on campus, much less in the sports arenas.

As Ashe moved on to high school, he continued to divide his energy between the classroom and the tennis court, spending summers with Dr. Johnson and as much time as he could manage during the rest of the year practicing at Brook Field and other courts in the area. Under Johnson's guidance he competed in the circumscribed tournaments then open to blacks. At the end of his junior year, Ashe faced a difficult decision and a unique opportunity—a turning point that would affect his future life and career.

His academic achievements had been superior. His tennis skills were still improving; he had won several regional titles and was ranked among the top junior players in the country. But Ashe had reached a frustrating plateau at age 17: he still could not enter and compete in white tournaments in Virginia, and he needed more competition and a chance to play during the winter months.

He and his father talked it out; they had often reasoned together. Arthur senior had provided his sons with firm discipline and a sense of responsibility that carried far beyond their years at home. He himself had been not only a hard worker but a real entrepreneur, a hustler, in the best sense of the word. As Arthur was growing up, his father continued his supervisory work in the Richmond Department of Recreation and eventually set up his own local landscaping and janitorial service; he came to own four houses in the area, in addition to the one he and the boys built in Gum Spring, 35 miles northwest of Richmond, where he now lives.

"Arthur," his father said in the summer of 1960, "there's a chance you could go out to St. Louis this year and live with a friend of Dr. Johnson's. What do you think?"

Ashe commented, "Daddy was a realist and knew there were few chances for a tennis player to make a living from his sport. He knew I needed someplace to play more in the winter." Johnson's friend, Richard Hudlin, a teacher at Sumner High School in St. Louis, offered to have Ashe live with his family during his senior year. Hudlin was a real tennis buff who had once been captain of the tennis team at the University of Chicago and had a tennis court in his own backyard. Arthur accepted the invitation with only a few misgivings, and the year in St. Louis gave him special opportunities to expand his tennis circles and also to grow and change in a new environment. "I came out of my shell," he recalled. "I could be anything I wanted in St. Louis ... and because I had a straight A average, I was often allowed to study on my own."

CHAPTER ONE

Ashe recalled with pride that Sumner had been "the first quality high school west of the Mississippi for blacks, with a very rich academic and athletic tradition." He found the course content and teaching quite comparable with that he had left at Maggie Walker, though he missed many friends with whom he had grown up.

During his senior year, Ashe polished his tennis skills with a wide range of players, including some of the top white competitors in St. Louis such as Chuck McKinley and Earl Buchholz. He practiced almost daily in the St. Louis Armory, where learning to adapt to the slick wooden floor with its fast skidding bounces gave a new dimension to his game. He would have become valedictorian of his class except that he had only attended the school for a year and was not eligible. Clearly, his voracious reading during childhood had given him a solid foundation for precollege studies, which continued to support him in his undergraduate years and military service.

In November 1960 Ashe won the U.S. Lawn Tennis Association's National Junior Indoors Tournament and gained additional recognition. During the Christmas holidays, he traveled to Miami Beach to play in another junior tournament and stopped in Richmond to visit his family. While at home, he received an unexpected telephone call from J. D. Morgan, the tennis coach at UCLA, a leading academic institution that had a top tennis program. Morgan offered him a scholarship to play tennis, and he accepted on the spot, without a moment's hesitation. "You could have knocked me over with a feather," Ashe said. "I had no idea UCLA had any interest in me."

The offer was a singular achievement that represented a milestone not only for Ashe, as a black player, but also for his coaches and supporters: Johnson, Hudlin, and Charity. They all recognized UCLA's stature as a university and as a tennis power. For Ashe it meant another big transition in his life, uprooting him once again, but providing him with the chance to move upward in both his education and career.

By the time Ashe graduated from high school, he was the fifth-ranked junior tennis player in the country and was named to the Junior Davis Cup team that traveled together in the summer of 1961. That kind of exposure moved the 17-year-old into a wider national spotlight and intensified the difficulties of being both a "star" black athlete and a role model of academic excellence. He felt the pressures of his unique status in tennis as he traveled and played around the United States and abroad. Often in the early 1960s the only other black people he saw were waiters, gardeners, and bus boys.

Later, from the perspective of more than 20 years of world travel from Soweto to Sydney and association with a wide range of people from tennis pros to prime ministers, Ashe thought back about the transition to UCLA, bridging the gap between Broad Street in Richmond to Wilshire Boulevard and Westwood. The expansive modern campus opened up new worlds for him; it was almost in sight of the posh homes and country clubs of Bel Air and Beverly Hills, yet it was also only a half-hour drive from the black and Hispanic ghettos in Watts and East Los Angeles.

Academically, at least, he had felt prepared for the change, yet, "I flunked the English examination upon entering college. I was dumbfounded," he said recalling the perils of the Subject A test. "But I quickly recovered; I breezed through the remedial course and went on into regular English the second semester. I never had any problems after that," he noted. And, after a pause, he added, "Yes, I did have one D, in statistics, which rattled me."

Tennis coach J. D. Morgan assumed a role in Ashe's life similar to that held earlier by Johnson and Hudlin. He became more than coach, however, and gave Ashe important personal help and guidance in preparing him for the demands

CHAPTER ONE

of undergraduate studies on top of athletic practice and travel. And, as a white man, he helped Ashe recognize some of the inconsistencies in white–black relationships that persisted even in the seemingly liberal southwestern corner of California. Blacks were not always welcome at certain clubs, though, contrarily, Ashe was invited within a year or two to play with Hollywood stars on their own courts.

Early in his freshman year, Ashe and Morgan discussed his academic program. "Arthur," the coach said, "this is a tough school academically, so don't get behind. . . . You're going to be here four years—all my boys graduate—so don't waste your time. Plan ahead, and let me know if you need help." Ashe had considered majoring in engineering or architecture, but Morgan suggested that business administration might be a better choice in light of the study and time demands, and in the end more useful to him. Ashe decided to take Morgan's advice, a decision that later proved sound.

Ashe had a good time at UCLA and found the liberal-arts training invaluable in later years as he traveled and followed new career opportunities apart from tennis. But he also had some lonely times and disappointments, particularly Christmas of his sophomore year. He stayed on campus during the holiday because he was short of money, and his Christmas dinner consisted of a sandwich and fruit from a dormitory vending machine.

While at UCLA, Ashe made a number of lasting friendships among whites, blacks, and Asians—men and women—who made up the amalgam of students on campus. Despite his intense concentration on academic studies and tennis in both high school and college, Ashe had a number of close friends in these years and by no means led a Spartan life. He liked going to parties, eating good food, and dating attractive women—tastes that later shaped his lifestyle as he began to travel the international professional tennis circuit during the 1970s. His close friends at UCLA included his roommate Jean

Baker, who was a black student from Haiti, and Charlie Pasarell from Puerto Rico, who was also on the tennis team.

Later he formed a close personal and business relationship with Donald Dell, a leading figure in the development of professional tennis. Dell is an urbane lawyer with degrees from Yale University and the University of Virginia Law School. He is also an excellent tennis player, and his combined knowledge of law, business, and sports has served his clients well.

Though Ashe's view of the world was influenced by his early years in Virginia, and he regarded himself as an underdog, he found that college life and experiences gave him new perspectives on the social and racial problems of the country and the world beyond.

Ashe moved toward graduation at UCLA after building a national reputation on the tennis courts (he won the NCAA singles and doubles titles in 1965 and helped the United States win the Davis Cup). But he also faced some personal decisions as the Vietnam War escalated and the likelihood that he might be drafted into the service increased. "Since I was 1-A, I decided I really didn't want to join the army as a private," Ashe recalled. "And I had some guidance from J. D. Morgan and Bob Kelleher (the Davis Cup captain at the time). They both urged me to extend my ROTC commitment and seek a commission." Ashe's father also agreed, since there was a family tradition of military service, including Arthur's brother, John, who was a career marine officer. Besides, Ashe reasoned, an officer's commission would look good on a résumé and would give him an additional option after college.

Shortly after graduating from UCLA in 1966, Ashe was sent to summer ROTC camp at Fort Lewis, Washington. After six weeks of training, he received his commission as a second lieutenant. That fall he was assigned to the U.S. Military Academy in West Point, New York, where he worked as a data-processing officer and could utilize some of his academic

CHAPTER ONE

training. He was also named assistant tennis coach at the academy, and for the next two years he enjoyed the best of two worlds, advancing his tennis career while serving the army in a positive and visible way through travel and personal appearances.

Ashe, like countless other young people, faced considerable pressures in the growing turbulence of the late 1960s as civil-rights activism and controversy over the Vietnam War intensified. The decade was marked by the assassinations of President John F. Kennedy in 1963, and of his brother, Robert, and of Martin Luther King, Jr., in 1968. While Ashe was at West Point the first of over 50,000 American servicemen died in Vietnam. Ashe remembered, "There was a funeral almost every day at West Point—I was saddened to see so many young men dead."

As an increasingly visible black athlete and army officer, Ashe disciplined himself to walk the proper but difficult path he believed in, faithful to his personal commitments and military duties. Events of these times regularly and inevitably touched his life, and later affected his travels, his career, his whole outlook on life. The prospect of a professional tennis career seemed uncertain to Ashe during this period, and when he completed his military service in 1968, the ferment within tennis circles was growing. The prospect of lucrative contracts and expanding income from television and advertising accelerated the campaign to merge amateur and professional tennis and to create "open" tournaments around the world.

Fortunately for Ashe, these developments came just as another stage of his life culminated with his victory in the U.S. Open Championship at Forest Hills, New York, in 1968. On a day in early September, he defeated Tom Okker of the Netherlands for the championship, and then stood with his father at his side to accept the trophy that was symbolic of the country's best tennis player, black or white. It was a high point on the long climb that had begun almost 20 years earlier on the courts of Brook Field. But winning the U.S. Open was only the first of many milestones in Ashe's career. A number of other major victories lay ahead, including the 1975 title at Wimbledon, where he defeated fellow American Jimmy Connors. During the late 1960s and early 1970s he moved on to become a top competitor among the expanding numbers of professional tennis players, winning the WCT and other championships throughout the world.

In 1970, under the sponsorship of the U.S. Department of State, Ashe made a goodwill tennis tour to South Africa, with another professional player, Stan Smith, and an entourage of writers and filmmakers. This trip, and others that Ashe made later, gave him an entirely new realization and understanding of the compelling racial and social problems facing that part of Africa, and he saw with stunning clarity scenes of exclusion, prejudice, and fear that evoked many personal memories. On subsequent trips to South Africa, Ashe met with both black and white leaders to discuss the problems there, and in his travels around the United States he came to know and work with civil-rights leaders toward positive solutions to this country's own racial problems. He did not become a militant, or, as he put it, "a sign carrier," but worked in his own constructive and effective ways—and continues to—in educational and counseling activities.

A serious heart attack in August 1979 ended Ashe's days of competitive tennis, but not his many related contributions to the sport and to the black community. He went on to become a shrewd businessman, coach of the U.S. Davis Cup team, journalist, broadcaster, and the subject of TV specials, films, and biographies.

At the end of a recent busy day at the ProServ sports-management office Ashe packed up a leather briefcase with homework. He planned to spend some time in the evening reviewing the nearly completed draft of his three-book project *A Hard Road to Glory*, delineating the full story of blacks in American sports. "It has occupied me for three years now,"

CHAPTER ONE

he said. "I'm pleased with it." He was also enthusiastic about his continuing contacts with a new generation of young people—and intensely aware of the complex problems facing them, particularly those who want to excel both academically and in sports.

As part of his work as a member of the Board of Directors of Aetna Life and Casualty Company, Ashe regularly meets with college students and offers practical advice on the "real world," careers and job opportunities. He also spends a lot of time visiting high schools and colleges around the country. February, which is black history month, is always a particularly busy time for him on this circuit.

Yet for all his worldwide commitments, he still remembers his roots and family ties in Virginia and makes regular trips to visit his father and perhaps do a little hunting or some fishing in the streams of rural Louisa County.

Among the celebrities, politicians, and corporate leaders with whom Ashe is involved in his everyday life, he keeps a special place for the small group of friends from that remarkable class of 1961. He had blocked out three days on his busy calendar to participate in their twenty-fifth reunion in July, at a gathering coordinated by one of the classmates, Carolyn Rowe Benson. "She's a remarkable woman," Ashe noted. "A champion swimmer—and yet she has one paralyzed arm."

So Arthur Ashe made one more sentimental journey to Richmond to join friends of another time. The old playground and tennis courts at Brook Field are long gone; a new post office has replaced them. The house on Sledd Street has been razed, and Maggie Walker High School has been transformed into a middle school. But the memories remain.

And not too many blocks away, next to the new baseball stadium of the Richmond Braves, stands one of the city's most modern indoor sports facilities, the Arthur Ashe, Jr., Athletic Center.

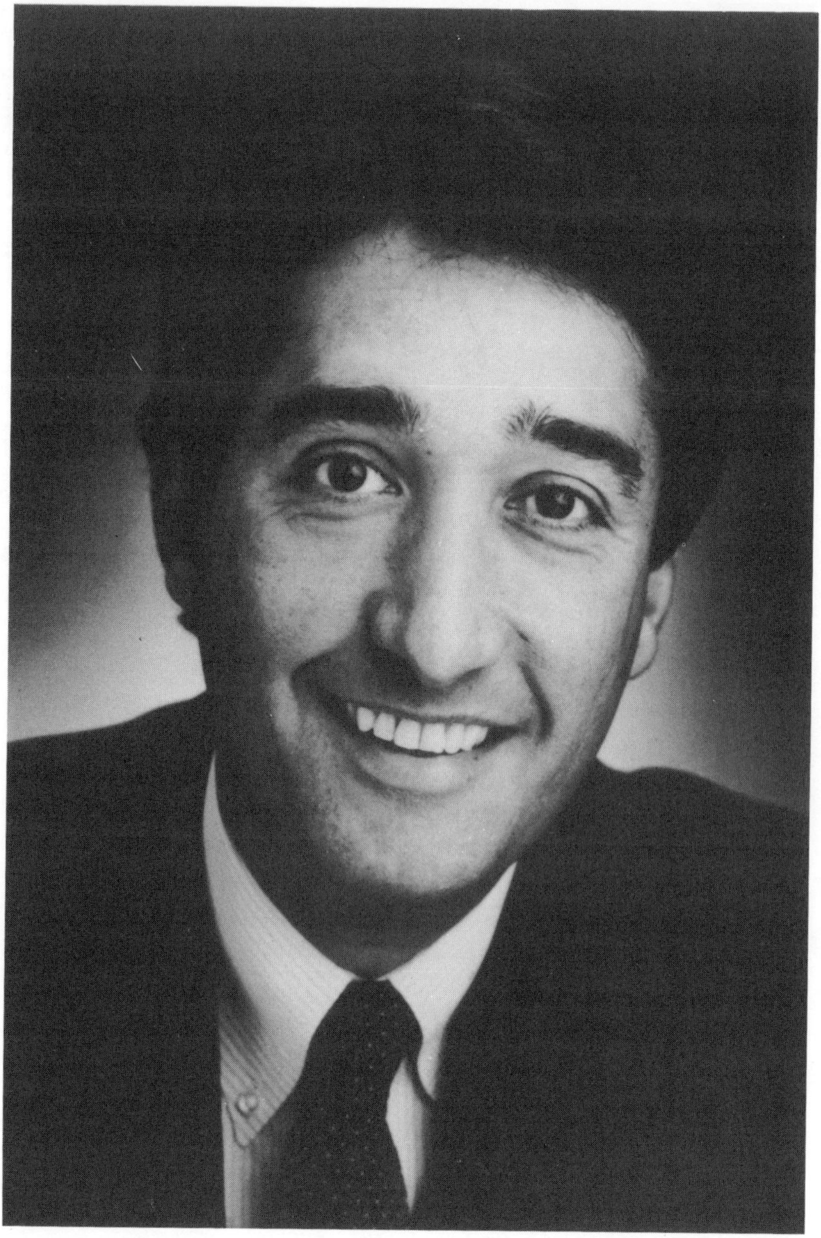

Chapter 2

HENRY CISNEROS

The sun had set three hours earlier, but the superheated, soggy night air of early August still pressed heavily on the tall, solitary figure in white shorts, T-shirt, and running shoes as he jogged easily along the flat asphalt streets on the western edge of San Antonio.

He absorbed the sights and sounds of his childhood as he ran through the nearly deserted streets, past the scrubby palms and neatly trimmed lawns, past the random wire and wood fences and the aging cars and pickup trucks in driveways. He sensed rather than smelled the lingering odors of simmering rice and chicken, herbs and spices and beans. And on the horizon a mile or two to the east he saw the lights and towers of the modern city that he was helping to build.

He was in a neighborhood of modest one-family homes with small yards, the area where he grew up and went to school. He still visited regularly and had a glass of iced tea and a piece of his mother's special lime chiffon pie after his late evening runs that helped him relax and forget some of the burdens of the long, troublesome days at the office.

CHAPTER TWO

But that night he ran on past his parents' white frame house. They had bought it with a few thousand dollars scraped together from savings and army pay at the end of World War II and had been living in it for some 40 years, raising five children. He continued toward his own place, not many blocks away, because he had another busy schedule tomorrow.

For Henry Cisneros there has been no question of returning to his roots. He never left. With his wife and two daughters, he lives in a simple but comfortable home built by his grandfather, Romulo Mungia.

On most days he drives himself to work in his 1972 Volkswagen. It's not far to his office, and on the way he travels the same streets where he runs, streets whose very names convey the bicultural nature of the city—Monterey to Zarzamora, across to Commerce, underneath Interstate 10 to the Plaza de Armas. Cisneros is as much a part of the town and its blended Mexican and American heritage as he is of the establishment that he directs as *alcalde*—mayor—of San Antonio, Texas, the nation's tenth largest city.

Just one generation ago it was highly unlikely—probably unthinkable—that a Mexican American would aspire to the mayor's office, much less be elected. In fact, just one generation ago, as a boy of 10, Henry's father, George Cisneros, was spending his days digging beets out of a Colorado field until he resolved to be the first in his family of 12 who would finish high school. He did more than that. He was one of only three Hispanics in his class to graduate, and he went to business school on a scholarship, studied hard for the civil-service exam and received the region's highest grade. He worked for the Bureau of Indian Affairs in New Mexico before entering the army, and served nearly three years in the South Pacific.

In the postwar years he combined civil-service and army duty to become chief of staff of the Ninetieth Army Reserve and retire as a colonel. The determination and initiative of George Cisneros carried him through this distinguished career. "I was prepared to work harder and longer than anyone else to succeed," he once told Henry. His respect for hard work and education was passed on undiminished to each of his three sons and two daughters, motivating all of them to graduate from college and move on to professional jobs in journalism, architecture, biomedical research, government, and music.

Henry chose to follow the paths of teaching and public service, and while he was still in his thirties he was well on his way to remarkable successes in both careers. Combining graduate study with fellowships and grants, Cisneros had received a master's degree from Texas A & M, an M.A. in public administration from Harvard, and a Ph.D. in public administration from George Washington University. He had been invited to speak at state and national political conventions, and to appear on such TV programs as *60 Minutes* and the *Today* show. In 1984 he was under serious consideration as a candidate for vice-president of the United States on the Democratic ticket.

In 1974 he returned to San Antonio to take a teaching position at the University of Texas campus there, and also to plunge into local politics. At the age of 27, he was elected the youngest councilman in the city's history. It was another of his many firsts, but as he told one audience, "I'm not interested in being the *first* anything. I just want to be the *best* I can be."

By 1981 he was ready to run for mayor, and he won in a spirited race. He was called a "barrio populist" but he spoke the language of the Sun Belt businessmen, too, and he won handily with some 62 percent of the vote. In 1983 he was reelected with an overwhelming 94 percent of the vote, gaining further regional and national prominence.

So the eldest son of George Cisneros demonstrated his

CHAPTER TWO

remarkable skills in political leadership and human relations, and came to govern his own city of more than 800,000, a city whose population is about 54 percent Hispanic.

San Antonio has a colorful and violent past, often mirroring the life and times of its famous monument, the Alamo, and the long interrelationships between Texans and Mexicans, both native to the land. Memories remain of Colonel Travis and Santa Anna, of Goliad, and of revenge at San Jacinto. Every few years someone produces a new film or book about the place, reviving again the feelings of pride and determination, of resolution and disappointment.

But the city is much more than memories. With its universities and military bases, it has become a magnet for new business and industry—high tech. Some eight million tourists come each year from all over the world to stroll the graceful Paseo del Rio that winds through the heart of downtown, or to visit museums devoted to Southwest history, culture, and art. The city treasures each chapter of its rich history, but it's anxious, too, about the present and the future, about the weaknesses of an oil-based economy.

In August 1986 the people of San Antonio made an important decision in the name of progress. In a special referendum, they voted two to one against a proposition that would have set rigid financial limits on spending and growth. The energy and vision of Mayor Cisneros helped carry the day.

A week or so later, on a sultry summer morning when the temperature was hovering in the nineties, he took time out from a full schedule to talk about his family, his school days, and his aspirations for the future.

His offices in city hall are temporarily relocated in the basement during renovation of the ornate pinkish tan sandstone building. Just outside, there is a new monument honoring the Hispanics in Texas "who through their pride and struggle have kept alive the heartbeat of Mexico, Texas' motherland, and in so doing have become an integral part of the culture and character of this proud state."

Henry Cisneros reflects that pride and history. He is a big man, an inch or so over six feet, and there's an air of Spanish nobility about his face—the sculptured cheekbones, the smooth tan skin, the deep-set dark brown eyes. On the day he was interviewed he relaxed on a comfortable sofa and discussed the economic challenges facing Texas and much of the Southwest. "One of the battlegrounds of the future will certainly focus on the economy—not just here, but in the country as a whole. I feel sure that America will develop in a way to serve the needs of all its people, to provide those vital ladders of opportunity that have given upward mobility to so many."

He was thinking perhaps of his father, and of his own dreams when he entered grade school speaking Spanish as a primary language, and knowing, somehow, that the scales of opportunity were still weighted against him—unless. . . .

He continued. "This feeling that everyone needs the opportunity to do better—to move up—that's the glue, the hope that holds society together. It's the thing that allows people to make a sacrifice today with the knowledge that it will pay off later."

A day earlier, Henry's mother Elvira had described the strong commitment of the Cisneros family to education. As motivator, organizer, and political consultant, she remembered that "we achieved by doing without other things if necessary. Together, we established our priorities, and we all worked hard to reach our goals. George and I knew that the only way the kids would accomplish what they needed to in life was through learning."

As the family grew and the children moved on to parochial schools, the budget was always tight. But there never was a sense of deprivation or a fear of poverty. Instead, there was confidence based on the careful and realistic balancing of resources against needs.

Continuing the interview, Mayor Cisneros reaffirmed the harmony and cohesion of their family. "I could never over-

CHAPTER TWO

emphasize the strength of our family unit" he said. "My mother was very much a disciplinarian; she set the highest standards for all of us."

"And while my father was not quite so driven, he was a strong believer in education—he had an abiding faith in it, as though by definition it would make your life better. He still reads widely, takes classes, teaches children. He was always reading—still is. I remember coming downstairs at 7 a.m. when I was a kid and my father had already been up for an hour reading."

Elvira Cisneros pointed out that each child had a special learning experience; for example, George, Jr., and Henry had both taken music lessons. George has become a recognized expert in ethnic and folk music, and is continuing his studies in electronic music at Ohio State University. "We devoted a lot of time each day in the summer to creative things . . . they had to write stories, act them out . . . do other things. They spent a lot of time at the neighborhood library, too. Henry read 30 or 40 books one summer. He loved school, never missed a day.

"During dinner, we often discussed current events, their school activities, and so on. And, from Sunday evening until Friday evening there was no TV. . . . That was a firm family rule . . . and it paid off."

From this supportive family environment, Henry moved easily through the early grades at the Church of the Little Flower elementary school. He quickly became fluent in English along with his first language, Spanish, and because of his advanced skills, the sisters included him in a group of bright classmates who skipped over the third grade.

Outside school, the Prospect Hill area of San Antonio was a pleasant community for kids in the 1950s. It was a mixed area of German and Hispanic families, just beyond the fringes of the west-end *barrio*. The neighborhood kids all played baseball and other games together, and Henry's high energy and leadership qualities began to shine through even then. "I was always fascinated with airplanes," he recalled. "I made models and read a lot about aviation history, speed records, wartime aces. Chuck Yeager and the X-15 people, the early astronauts, were among our heroes then."

As an undersized 14-year-old, Henry made the important transition to Central Catholic High School, a place whose rigorous discipline and solid academic curriculum had a strong positive impact on his thinking and intellectual development. His mentor, the genial and scholarly Brother Martin McMurtrey, who was his English teacher, also instructed him in much broader realms. The basic educational program was reinforced by the teaching of strong social ethics, and no doubt expanded Henry's humanistic sensitivity.

A handsome, three-story beige brick structure facing TV station KSAT on busy St. Mary's Street in downtown San Antonio, Central Catholic has been in its present location for some 50 years and serves now, as it did in Henry's day, as a springboard for the upwardly mobile. The original school was founded over a century ago in two rooms over a livery stable by the Marianist Brothers who came to Texas from Bordeaux after the French Revolution.

Inside the main entrance there is a permanent display of photographs of graduates dating to the late 1920s. In the second row of the class of 1964, a skinny, shyly smiling Henry Cisneros looks out between F. Catalani and R. Coindreau. His dark hair is closely cropped, and like the others he wears a white shirt and dark bow tie.

Brother Martin McMurtrey took time out from his summer research project to talk about Henry. McMurtrey is a ruddy-faced man of medium build with smooth skin and neatly trimmed gray hair. His eyes sparkle with the enthusiasm of a dedicated teacher. He lives with five other teaching brothers in a residence house on Camden Street, just behind the school's playing fields. McMurtrey has been on the faculty at Central for 30 years, and although he is nearing retirement age, he still carries on a vigorous program of teaching, study,

CHAPTER TWO

and volunteer work with inner-city students. He devotes several hours a week (time that must be borrowed from some inner reserve) to tutoring poor kids, black and Mexican, "who don't have the advantage of private school." He also teaches English to newly arrived aliens. "This is a labor of love," he said.

"In Henry's day," he recalled, "the school was somewhat smaller and not as expensive—not much over $100 a year for tuition. Now, of course, we have more than 800 students and the cost is more like $2,000 a year. But the basic concept and mission haven't changed. It's still a place where Mexican Americans—or anyone—can come to prepare for college.

"As an example," he continued, "I remember a janitor who worked here and also held a job at Providence [the adjacent girls' school]. His main aim in life was to make enough to put his kids through school here and give them a head start on college and a career. Well over 90 percent of our graduates go to college. But thinking about Henry, he was the first of the family to come here. I also taught his brothers, George and Tim. Henry was ambitious from the first day he arrived. He always read more than assigned, was intense, and had wide-ranging interests. Henry had four years of Latin. He read 9 or 10 Shakespeare plays and took all the math and science courses we offered, though math was not one of his strongest subjects.

"We moved him into advanced English when he was a sophomore. We could all see his potential. And even then he was an excellent extemporaneous speaker . . . one of the best I've ever heard."

Henry remembered the importance of learning the fundamentals at Central Catholic. "Studying Latin," he recalled, "gave me a stronger base for English. Latin is a very logical and rational language, almost mathematical in its precision. I know the analytical skills I learned then are still with me. Sometimes just for fun I try the *Reader's Digest* vocabulary test and usually get 18 out of 20—sometimes 20."

HENRY CISNEROS

The assassination of President John F. Kennedy in November 1963 remains a vivid memory for Henry Cisneros after more than 20 years. Just one day before the fatal shooting, he had walked with Brother McMurtrey and others a few blocks across town to watch the Kennedy motorcade in San Antonio. The subsequent events in Dallas and the funeral ceremonies in Washington shocked and moved the 16-year-old Henry and his classmates. After a requiem mass at the school, he composed a memorial poem that was included in the class anthology that year, and the whole experience left an indelible imprint on his early life.

Along with many other Mexican Americans, Henry and his family have always had a high regard for the Kennedys and their aspirations for the country. In fact, a quotation from Bobby Kennedy stands framed on Cisneros's desk today, and speaks eloquently to a political and perhaps personal kinship: "It is the shaping impulse of America that neither fate nor nature nor the irresistible tides of history, but the work of our own hands, matched to reason and principle that will determine destiny."

Henry moved toward high school graduation with a fine academic record and an impressive number of extracurricular activities: He had continued his early interest in music and played French horn in the band and had joined the school's ROTC unit, reflecting, no doubt, the influence of his father's career. At Central Catholic in those days there was no separate office for counseling and guidance. McMurtrey and others worked with Henry and his family in considering college options. Henry's first choice was the Air Force Academy, but because of his relatively young age and still-developing physique, he was given an alternate appointment and urged to spend another year maturing, perhaps in a military prep school.

That sounded more like a detour than a transition to Henry, and he decided instead to apply to Texas A & M University for the fall semester of 1964. He was accepted,

CHAPTER TWO

and a couple of months after his seventeenth birthday he made the first of many trips up to College Station. His experiences during his years there became among the most formative of his life. He learned the rigors of discipline as well as the demands and rewards of comradeship in A & M's Corps of Cadets, and the special spirit of the university, which generated a loyalty that he still cherishes. A little over 20 years later, he would be appointed a regent of Texas A & M and, as a member of its statewide governing board, would play an important role in developing plans and priorities for the institution.

But, as it is for many young people, being uprooted from his family, friends, and community and the challenge of new surroundings, new faces, new rules, was at the outset difficult for Henry Cisneros. He was one of very few Mexican Americans at the school, and there was latent and sometimes overt discrimination. His first roommate objected to rooming with him. The hours were long, the courses tough, the hazing and intimidation hard to cope with. "But I didn't get more than my share," Cisneros recalled. "It was a good experience for me. My character was shaped by those years as much as by anything else I've ever done. I was trained in and tested on accomplishment and merit. I learned that if you work you will attain. There's a real link between dedicating yourself to something 100 percent and then actually achieving it. I was determined that I would compete and survive."

Cisneros has since described the university as one of the last of the pure meritocracies, and as a student he began to realize that he could turn the environment and style of the place to his advantage.

While he mustered his inner strength, Henry was also sustained by his family. More than once during the early weeks at A & M they packed a picnic lunch and piled into the family car for the long, 300-mile round trip to visit with him for a few hours.

Henry not only survived under duress, he prospered. He

was twice named outstanding cadet in his ROTC unit, and by the end of his sophomore year was selected sergeant major of the Texas Aggie band.

About midway through his college career, Henry met Wayne Stark, who served for some 30 years as director of the Memorial Student Center and is now a special assistant to Texas A & M president Frank Vandiver. Stark is a dynamic, avuncular sort of man who, in addition to his other duties, made it his special mission at the university to spot, challenge, and encourage young men who he felt had unusual potential.

Stark remembered an early meeting with Cisneros. "He wanted to be considered for listing in a college *Who's Who* directory and he just barely lacked the necessary grade-point average. I told him he could be in the top group academically if he really tried. I said 'you have to get off your butt and go.' He told me he wouldn't need top grades if he went into the Army, as he expected to do. I told him that was baloney, that top grades meant the road to leadership in any field, the army included, and especially if he wanted to go to graduate school. That seemed to shake him up. From then on, his grades were outstanding, all A's and a few B's. And he kept up all of his other interests, too."

"Wayne was a remarkable force at an important time in my life," Cisneros said. "He still is. We keep in touch—he's sending me *his* new protégés now. He shaped up my academic work, helped me develop leadership skills, gave me opportunities to develop my speaking ability, and he rounded me out socially, too, by introducing me to business leaders through his network."

Stark focused on young Hispanics making their way through A & M, probably because he recognized they needed more supplemental help and reinforcement than other groups at the time. Today an impressive number of influential business and government leaders around the state and country proudly characterize themselves as "Stark's Boys"—

CHAPTER TWO

a sort of prairie mafia. Stark modestly admits that many of his Aggies now hold key jobs on Wall Street, Capitol Hill, and in top management firms. One writer attributes some of their success to "having the genes of the frontier people."

Through Stark and the Student Conference on National Affairs, Cisneros broadened his perspectives dramatically, traveling around the state on fund-raising and public-relations visits with business and government leaders, and going on to participate in national student seminars on the East Coast. He found that his career focus had begun to shift toward public service and urban affairs (though he majored in English).

Following his graduation, Henry carefully considered the alternatives of teaching or government service. He began to imagine that he could take his father's obsession with education a step further, and devote his own career to helping Mexican Americans overcome generations of poverty and educational neglect.

Studies by sociologists and educators were regularly documenting the statistical bad news. One U.S. Commission on Civil Rights report described "continuing patterns of racial isolation, diminished school holding power, relative paucity of college attendance. . . ." For every 100 Mexican Americans entering first grade in the late 1960s, only about 23 entered college and only 5 received a degree. For Anglos, the corresponding figures were 49 percent entering college and 24 percent completing a degree.

Cisneros was fortunate to receive a full scholarship for graduate study from the Texas Municipal League, and he decided to stay on a year at College Station to complete his master's degree, also working part time as an assistant to the city manager of nearby Bryan, Texas. From there, he returned to San Antonio to take a full-time job with the Model Cities program, and he married his high school sweetheart, Mary Alice Perez. The work brought him face to face with the essential problems of the inner city and taught him the day-to-day realities of local government.

During that year, he began to see more clearly that the basic, long-range problems of cities must be solved by the top levels of political leadership and that, while planners and executors were essential, his own skills and interests were perhaps more suited to the broader challenges of administration and finance. As he put it, "I wanted to learn finance, budget, and taxes . . . I decided I needed a degree in administration and finance."

He was accepted in the Ph.D. program of metropolitan urban administration at George Washington University in Washington, D.C., and moved there in 1970 with his wife, not certain how they would support themselves while he studied. Through a contact with an associate from the Model Cities Program, he landed a job as an administrative assistant with the National League of Cities, and Mary Alice took a job as a translator for the Riggs National Bank.

Henry's determination, high energy, and organizational skills carried him through yet another difficult transition, and he managed to satisfy the demands of his academic courses and research along with the long hours of a full-time job with the NLC. Washington was a perfect training ground for him. He became more and more engrossed as he began to see how the theoretical teachings of his graduate studies applied to the complex issues facing urban centers. He also came to realize that he might be able to pursue careers in both education and government and that at some point his own city of San Antonio could be the ideal place to begin.

For the next three years or so, Henry Cisneros's life continued to move ahead at the same intense pace. Against high odds, he won a prestigious White House Fellowship, competing against top applicants from around the country. In the course of the interviews, he once recalled, "I looked around me and saw a guy who was number one in his class at West

CHAPTER TWO

Point, a Rhodes scholar, people who had never lost a competition in their lives . . . I did not think I was going to make it."

But he did, and was assigned to work for the Secretary of Health, Education and Welfare, Elliot Richardson, who later served as Secretary of Defense and Attorney General in the Nixon Administration. In addition to being Cisneros's boss, Richardson was also, probably unknowingly, a personal and social model for the young Texan, who highly respected his intellectual honesty. He even began to emulate Richardson's Ivy League dress and lifestyle.

In an introduction to a 1984 book on Cisneros, Richardson says he was struck by Henry's intelligence and charm, "but what most impressed me was his air of quiet confidence—the outward reflection, I was sure, of an inner sense of balance. . . . I told him I regarded him as a 'national treasure,' alluding to his Hispanic American background."

Later, Richardson said, "Henry's performance has given new life to one of my favorite observations: Politics is the most difficult of the arts and the noblest of the professions."

"There is no doubt about it," Cisneros commented, "Elliot Richardson was one of the decisive influences in my life, pushing me toward public service. . . . He proved to me that it was an honorable, respectable profession; that the best in our society could reasonably spend a lifetime of productivity in that field."

In the course of his work with Richardson, Henry wrote Wayne Stark a letter of appreciation and reflected on that year "as a quantum leap for me . . . I only hope what I have contributed is a fraction of what I have learned . . . and I still appreciate the part you played in it all."

The White House fellows as a group had extensive opportunities to savor the Washington scene beyond their official duties. They attended all kinds of briefings and meetings and regularly went to luncheons, dinners, and receptions where they mingled with statesmen and journalists. Cisneros remembered meeting President Nixon, newsmen Marvin Kalb and Dan Rather, and economist Milton Friedman, among others. He called these experiences "a heady wine," and took a special delight in having his picture appear in the society section of the Washington *Post*. He told Stark, "This was probably the last place I ever thought I'd see a picture of this south Texas clod."

From Washington, it seemed a logical—perhaps necessary—step to Harvard, and the John F. Kennedy School of Government. With a grant from the Ford Foundation, he was able to complete another master's degree, this time concentrating on urban economic development and public-policy analysis. Characteristically, he also worked part time and took courses at MIT, where he was a teaching assistant.

Finally, in the summer of 1974, he and his wife completed (at least temporarily) the eastern cycle of their lives and headed back to San Antonio, where Henry had decided to take a teaching position at the University of Texas campus there.

It was at this juncture that one of his friends, writing to the A & M Former Students Association, reported on Henry's progress: "He has accepted a position at the U of T. . . . He will be teaching urban economics; and just between you and me, he will also be doing a lot of politicking. Someday Henry will be Texas's governor or senator."

Close. Within seven years he would be elected mayor, winning nearly two-thirds of the vote. But during the intervening period, he embarked on his academic teaching career and at the same time took on the rough and tumble politics of San Antonio. At age 27, he was elected to the city council, a position that broadened and deepened his understanding of the city's problems and of its potential.

A bit later in his career, he reflected on the elements forming his political base. First, he said he was able to convince people of his commitment to equality among Anglos and Mexican Americans. Second, because of his education

35

CHAPTER TWO

and experience he could successfully play the role of broker and arbiter among the forces and factions of the city. And third, he inevitably benefited from his ethnicity, noting, "There's a point where you stop being a curiosity or a novelty ... but you never lose some obvious attributes such as your color and your cultural background." However, he added, "You must work with equal integrity to make the system work for those who have been outside the economic mainstream." This was an echo of the Kennedys, perhaps, and of his own father striving for a high school diploma, the passport that would take him out of the beet fields.

By the time Cisneros ran his first mayoral race in 1980, he had become a fairly well-known figure around Texas and in the East, where he maintained his contacts along the Boston-to-Washington axis. But in his campaign he faced formidable opposition from John Thomas Steen, a three-term councilman and prosperous businessman with a solid war record and extensive personal and party resources behind him. Steen represented much of the San Antonio establishment and represented it well, having been active in a variety of social and civic organizations.

Henry, on the other hand, had few tangible resources at the outset, but a great reservoir of determination, plenty of energetic volunteers, and, eventually, support from important members of the business community.

Though he had professional help along the way, Henry attributed much of his success to the homegrown aspects of his campaign, which were directed by his younger brother George and by his mother, who traveled ceaselessly through the neighborhoods on behalf of her son. Henry had learned, either through intuition or training, how to campaign, and he did it well. He could—and did—appeal to many constituencies. As his mother aptly put it, "Henry has caring qualities, call it charisma if you will. People recognize that and they respond."

Wayne Stark also speaks of those qualities, the magnetism. "We knew when he left here that he was going to be somebody very special wherever he went. He just had that extra spark, a natural warmness. He relates to people, he's open and very honest."

After winning the election with a little over 62 percent of the vote, Cisneros moved ahead to carry out programs that he had supported as a councilman, and most important, he seemed able to bridge some of the differences between the Anglo and Hispanic communities, generating a new sense of unity and pride around town.

Improving education and widening opportunities for Mexican Americans and blacks remained a high priority. With the support of a $1 million private foundation grant, he personally joined school and college leaders in 1981 to develop and implement a pioneering program, Options for Excellence, for the earlier identification and guidance of able students. The success of this work in San Antonio has encouraged other cities like Albuquerque to use it as a model.

He was no longer viewed as a curiosity or a flash in the pan, not by San Antonians or by a much wider segment of the American public who had increasing opportunities to see and hear him on national television and in appearances on college campuses. How did he establish his political success as mayor? He noted that he had to demonstrate not only ability, but also responsibility. "One of the hardest tasks was to prove to the business community that I was not bent on wild spending or fiscal mismanagement. . . . I wanted to show we could manage as responsibly and prudently as anyone else. And we had to show that we were better at delivering services—leaner, tougher, better than anybody."

Since his base pay is only $50 per week (for being a member of the city council), Cisneros derives a good share of his income today from the salary he receives for being a faculty member at Trinity University, which he supplements

CHAPTER TWO

with substantial lecture and speaking fees, and frequent appearances on network features and talk shows like *60 Minutes*, the morning shows, and *Larry King Live*.

Cisneros has all the tools now: the background, the experience, the desire to do almost anything he wants. As he sat in the mayor's office halfway through a summer's day, he began to contemplate the rest of his schedule and to plan for the remainder of the week. He would have a working lunch and make the keynote address at a three-day conference on the problems and prospects of the Southwest. He would meet with his staff to discuss the almost infinite and seemingly constant requests by individuals and groups to meet with him—as soon as possible. Late in the day, he would join his wife and daughters who had come into town for dinner.

He remains a patient man, visionary but practical; a long-range planner who strives for rational and achievable goals, a master of shaping consensus. Despite the financial restraints and inhibitions facing the Southwest in the late 1980s, he has strong faith in the area's people and in its potential, its ability to grow and develop.

Where does Henry Cisneros go from here? The odds suggest that he will play out the next phase of his life on a much larger stage. He is already a recognized leader among mayors of major cities. His future could lie in Austin at the state capitol or in the governor's mansion. He may aspire to the U.S. Congress, or welcome a high government post in Washington. Whatever his course, it seems certain that his foundations in church and family will sustain him as they have in the past. As his mother has noted, "Henry has had many blessings in his life . . . and you should not discount God's will. Despite all his success, Henry retains his humility."

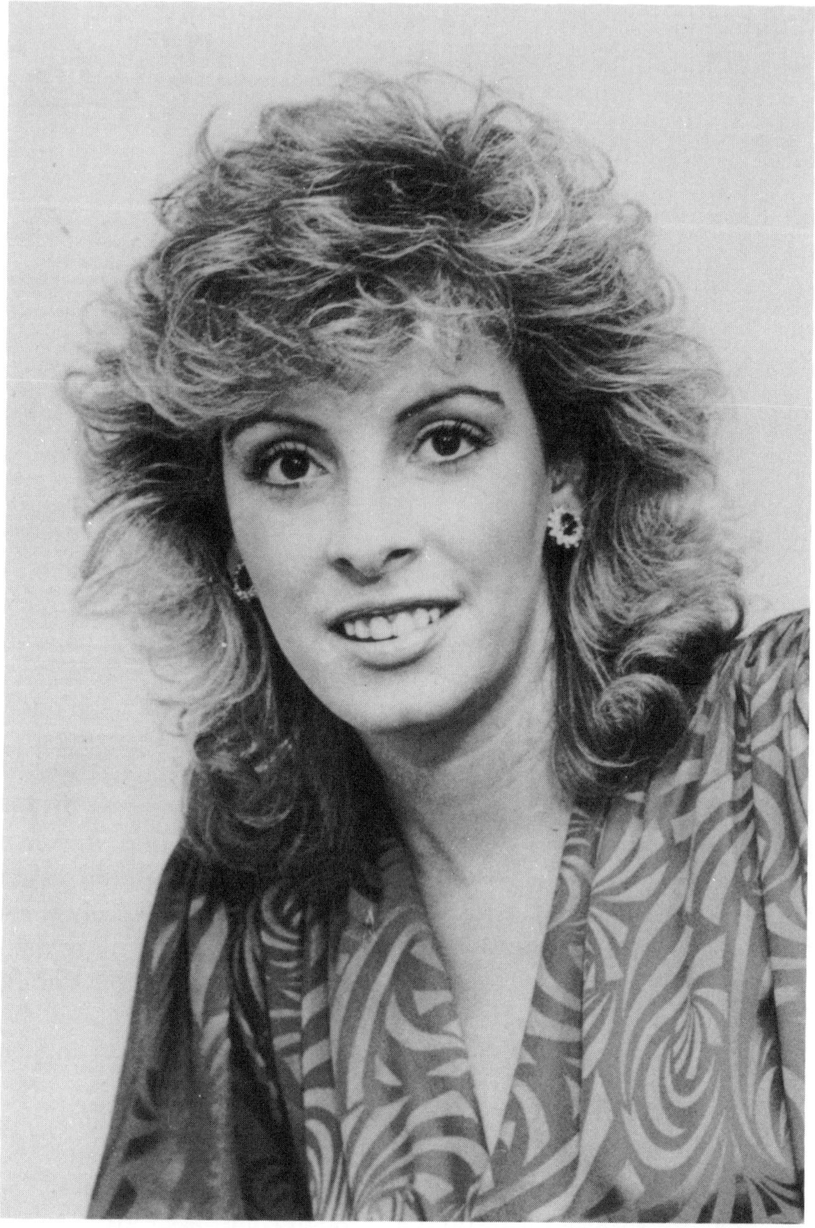

Chapter 3

KAREN HALL

One of the most influential people in the entertainment world today is a slender and attractive young blonde named Karen Hall, who writes for a living. Her office is tucked away among a jumble of ramshackle sets, make-believe buildings, and monolithic sound stages on the Twentieth Century Fox lot on West Pico Boulevard in Los Angeles.

Although she has just passed her thirtieth birthday, Karen is an eminently successful veteran in the fiercely competitive field of television writing. Her work for programs like *M*A*S*H* and *Hill Street Blues* has won her three Emmy nominations and numerous Writer's Guild awards, and she is one of the most respected and sought-after members of her profession.

Her stories for the widely acclaimed *M*A*S*H* series reach worldwide audiences through syndication, and the show's fans still faithfully follow the antics of Hawkeye, Radar, and Margaret Houlihan through countless reruns.

CHAPTER THREE

In the fall of 1986, Karen moved another notch up the ladder, assuming the prestigious and challenging position of supervising producer of the popular offbeat detective series *Moonlighting*.

Hall is one of a small number of women who have succeeded in television production. Women direct only 10 percent of all TV shows and write only 17 percent of prime-time shows. But Karen never doubted that she would make it.

She began writing in grade school, published essays and stories in the high school paper and honor society magazine, and wrote stories and plays with her sister and other collaborators. In college she formalized her training, taking playwriting courses that gave discipline and structure to her work, and more important, gave her a chance to see her words come to life on a stage.

One warm July morning, Karen took time out from planning the fall shooting schedule for *Moonlighting* to talk about her family, her schooling, and the development of her career.

Despite the hectic pace of dawn-to-dusk (or later) filmmaking, Karen seemed relaxed and accustomed to the pressures, and she talked confidently about her first encounters with Hollywood. She was dressed casually in California work clothes—a long black skirt, white blouse, green sweater-vest, and white boots. Her pale gold hair was cut short and her brown eyes lightly accented with blue eyeshadow.

"I remember first visiting Los Angeles way back in the summer of 1977," she said, as though it were the Dark Ages. "It was part of a seminar trip, and two important things happened for me, aside from seeing how films and TV shows were actually made.

"First, I got some sample scripts to study for format and style, but more important, I met Earl Hamner. He gave me invaluable advice about this whole business, and he also tried to be realistic. He warned me that each year hundreds of writers—good writers—come to California to break in, and that only two or three make it."

Karen laughed. "I still remember my response. I said 'good, that means two others besides me.' I guess I was a little brash then, but I always had confidence in my ability."

Karen was born in Chatham, Virginia, and went through public schools there. The town lies nestled among rolling green hills—tobacco country—sparsely settled, bucolic, a continent and a world away from the tumult of the Twentieth Century Fox lot on West Pico.

Main Street is pretty much the core of the one-stoplight town some 150 miles southwest of Richmond. It is a narrow thoroughfare, bordered by graceful shade trees, bounded to the west by the imposing buildings of Hargrave Military Academy and to the east by fashionable Chatham Hall School for Girls.

Downtown is the essence of small town America, and you keep waiting for Opie to run out from Floyd's barber shop or perhaps John-Boy to park his Model A Ford at the curb in front of the general store. Above the whir of cicadas on a summer's day, you half expect to hear the sound of 76 trombones and to see Professor Harold Hill's band turn the corner at any moment.

Chatham seems to be a nice place to grow up and maybe even a better place to dream about escaping from to a fantasy world, as Karen Hall and her sister Barbara did, sitting up half the night talking and writing in their second-story bedroom in the family's tan frame house on Main Street, opposite the Presbyterian Church.

How do writers learn? Are they born or made? What do they need to study in school—and for how long? In Karen's case, the basic elements and building blocks of human experience and emotion began to take shape in her mind as she moved through school and came of age in Chatham. She subconsciously began to blend her own extensive reading of biographies, fiction, and poetry with her family's dedication to learning and excellence, and to develop her own special gifts.

CHAPTER THREE

The sights, sounds, and personalities of Karen's town flowed into her memory bank to be drawn on and merged with thoughts and places of her own invention. Qualities of tenacity and quiet confidence came to the surface, coupled with a ready wit, a developing sense of dramatic skill, and a keen perception of speech rhythms and behavioral traits marking or defining character.

Somehow, Chatham provided her with a sense of universality that would later touch her television work in various ways. The cattle barns and sheds beyond the town could have been translated into the imagined atmosphere of Radar's family farm in Iowa. Some of the traditional ideals and philosophies of Virginians were similar to those of Hawkeye Pierce's father in Crab Apple Cove, Maine. And the southern cavalry tradition may have been passed on (a couple of generations later) to Colonel Sherman Potter.

As Karen talked about her own writing and the influences on it, she remembered lazy summer days when she first discovered the poetry of John Keats, and later years when she began to listen carefully to the compelling messages of Bruce Springsteen. "It's almost impossible for me to say exactly where an idea or a line of dialogue came from," she said. "There's as much of Keats in my work as there is Springsteen or John Steinbeck. It may have been just one word or phrase they expressed so well that moved something in me, and enabled me to use it later in a special way in a script."

During my visits to the Chatham area, Karen's parents and her high school English teacher, Elsie Todd, talked with me about her family background, education, and early determination to be a writer.

"Karen's roots go deep into the southern heritage," her mother Flo said. "She may have gotten her writing ability from my side of the family. Granddaddy wrote a history book and I believe it's in the Library of Congress. Our family goes way back in this state. I think we qualify for the FFV [First

Families of Virginia, whose origins date to the founding years 1607–24]—Karen looked it up once."

"We didn't have much of a library at home," Karen's father Ervis recalled, "but Karen and her sister Barbara made a lot of trips to the town library in Chatham. It was also the Pittsylvania County Library, and pretty good. Karen was always over there, and she kept it up in the summer, too, with their reading programs and competitions."

"Karen was always reading and writing from the time she was very young," her mother recalled. "She read so much I don't know how she still has eyes to see. And she never believed she couldn't be a writer, and a top writer at that! Her philosophy was 'if anybody can do it, I can do it better.' Karen always wanted to be the best."

Her determination had an aggressive edge to it. Her former teacher Elsie Todd said, "Karen was extremely talented, and she had an inventive mind. She spent lots of time alone, in a fantasy world with her books and stories. She was highly motivated—self-motivated—and while she was involved in lots of school activities, she didn't have many close friends. The other kids knew she had something they didn't have, and they were jealous."

"Maybe it was more misunderstanding than jealousy," Karen speculated. "I listened to my own drummer. I guess I was a loner. And even though my folks thought I was a little weird, they always supported me and my plans to the utmost. My parents always worked hard and believed in excellence. They passed this on to my sister, Barbara, and to me, and they were always involved in our schools."

From the early days, it almost seemed as though there were two Karen Halls, or, more accurately, two aspects to her own personality. There was the public Karen and the private one. The public Karen appeared first, captured in the family scrapbook at age seven, with long blond curls, playing an angel in the first-grade nativity pageant. The following

CHAPTER THREE

year she came in second in the broad jump and sack race and joined the second grade's 100 percent attendance group. She studied ballet and dance, and her sixth-grade class photo shows a smiling Karen in the second row among about 30 others. An easily recognizable portrait of General Robert E. Lee looks down sternly from the classroom wall.

By 1973 Karen and a black friend were co-captains of the high school cheerleaders. A yearbook photo shows them trim and athletic, resplendent in their sweaters and short pleated skirts, holding pompons. The public Karen also won the district championship in extemporaneous speaking and was listed in *Who's Who Among American High School Students*. The next year she became one of nine top honor graduates in the county. She was immersed in class activities—Tri Hi-Y, Beta Club, Future Teachers—and she helped edit the yearbook.

But meantime, the private Karen had grown and prospered, too, stocking a rich imaginary world through reading, writing, and inventing. She and Barbara took up the guitar and wrote songs. She and a pen pal in Chicago collaborated in writing plays.

At an early age, television had an impact on Karen. "I do remember thinking how there was this box in the living room that you could turn on and it would tell you a story. It seemed incredible to me at the time, and I guess I've never stopped feeling that way."

The medium was important for her, but perhaps not as much as the message that it carried. "I used to watch the credits when I got older," she said. "I used to say 'one day my name will be up there.'" Karen laughed as she sat in her offices in the heart of the Twentieth Century Fox dream factory where she writes and produces stories that now reach millions. "These days I am asking 'why isn't my name bigger on the screen, and why doesn't it stay on longer?'"

"We did watch the *Osmonds*, I remember," Karen said, "but not a whole lot else. Except *The Waltons*, of course. Since it was about Virginians and a part of the state not too far from Chatham, we watched it." The influence seemed to grow. "I remember seeing the program one night when John-Boy was writing on his yellow pad. *I* used a yellow pad. And he was striving to be a writer. Then it came to me that there has to be a real writer, writing this show, and that he was from Virginia. It turned out, of course, to be Earl Hamner."

Karen continued, "I watched the show because I wanted to be a writer. I didn't become a writer as a *result* of watching. I said to myself, 'boy, this could happen! I could do this!' "

In her high school English class, Karen wrote an essay on Virginia customs as portrayed in Hamner's original story "Spencer's Mountain". With a bit of encouragement and technical help from Mrs. Todd ("Karen was a little weak on spelling . . . we cleaned the paper up a bit"), Karen sent the essay to Hamner and got back a handwritten note of thanks and appreciation. Her inherent skill and demonstrated initiative had opened a tiny doorway of opportunity that she would explore a few years later when she went to Hollywood.

Karen remembers Chatham High as a comfortable school, but one not distinguished by its academic excellence. She was in school from 1970–74, when the countywide integration of public schools was taking place—a time of uneasiness and uncertainty, but little overt disturbance or violence. There was a distinct vocational orientation to the curriculum and the goals of the administration essentially mirrored the wants and needs of the community. Less than half of Karen's graduating class went on to college; most of those who did opted for the nearby community college or business school. Many of her friends took jobs in Chatham or nearby Danville, and still live in the area.

The school is a modern, flatroofed, red-and-tan, brick-and-glass structure, designed to be efficient and durable. There's a large multipurpose lunchroom downstairs; rows of metal lockers flank the halls; and an airy library occupies a spacious corner on the second floor. Most of the 800 students

CHAPTER THREE

ride the bus to school, as Karen did, approaching along the ridge south of town and turning west at Tightsqueeze Corners.

In addition to her immersion in cheerleading, debating, and honor society activities, Karen followed the regular college preparatory curriculum, concentrating on establishing a base for her future teaching plans. "Guidance at the school was not really strong," Elsie Todd recalled. "Some of the teachers had to give special attention to the best college-bound students and help them prepare for the transition. Now, at least, the school has an Advanced Placement program, and the county has developed a good program for the gifted, so things are improving," she added.

Though neither of Karen's parents had gone to college, both were intensely interested and involved in the education of their daughters, throughout their schooling. When Karen was in high school, her mother worked in a local store and also at the Hargrave Academy as part of the Halls' effort to build up college funds. She served on PTA groups and became a cheerleader sponsor.

Elsie Todd remembered Flo Hall's active role. "She instilled a sense of values and pride in the girls," she said. "And Ervis Hall also provided great encouragement and support to Karen as she moved through high school." Once, when Karen brought home an F in a math class because of an alleged absence, her father probed into the situation and found the teacher had inadvertently marked her absent on a snow day when the whole school was closed. A minor, isolated incident perhaps, but one indicative of parental concern.

"There was a genuine closeness in the family," Mrs. Todd said. "Ervis was determined that Karen would have good teachers; there was no doubt in his mind that she would go on to college and be a great success.

"Karen herself had an inner strength, an inventive mind, a unique gift for analyzing poetry and plays. She could perceive the direction and meaning of a poem better than anyone I have taught . . . better than most college students. I guess my main contribution to Karen's success was that I did not kill her creativity. As her career progressed, Karen was fortunate to be in the right place at the right time to make a break. Note, I say *make*, not get . . . she did it for herself. She had a kind of subtle aggression, and that did alienate some people."

Later, Karen would write Mrs. Todd a note of thanks "for all your help, all the knowledge and appreciation of literature that you gave me."

That dedication was demonstrated during the summer of Karen's senior year, when Mrs. Todd arranged a special English class for two or three of her best English students to help them bridge the gap to college. "It was the kind of enrichment that I knew they needed," she recalled. "They hadn't had either the time or the opportunity in regular classes to broaden their knowledge of literature and drama. We covered a whole range of authors, including James Joyce. I remember that Karen identified with the struggles and aspirations of Stephen Dedalus in the *Portrait of the Artist as a Young Man*."

Despite her excellent school record and many outside activities, Karen's transition to college did not follow a smooth course, though it was characteristic of her independent spirit. It was also when her private and public worlds began to blend, partly as a result of her own maturity, and partly because of social and academic realities closing in on her.

Decisions about going to college are made in strange and unpredictable ways, sometimes based as much on impulse, whim, and courage as on grade-point averages, test scores, and wisdom drawn from handbooks. In Karen's case, the stage had been set some six years earlier during a family trip. The Halls frequently took the girls on summer travels around Virginia, and to Washington, D.C., and the Carolinas. One

CHAPTER THREE

year, when Karen was about 12, they visited Colonial Williamsburg and the adjacent College of William and Mary. Karen was fascinated by the school and decided she would go to college there. She stuck with this decision and never even applied anywhere else, violating all of the rules of prudent planning and admissions gamesmanship.

During a subsequent visit to the college and an orientation session for prospective students, an assistant dean of admissions suggested to Karen and her parents that she would probably not be admitted because of her academic record and SAT scores. "She never did well under pressure," her mother recalled. "She wasn't good on standardized tests." Elsie Todd agreed. "No doubt she was very bright, but she preferred essay exams."

Even when the letter came, Karen refused to accept her rejection. She promptly organized a letter-writing campaign to the college. Mrs. Todd joined her. Karen wrote personally, and apparently with great persuasion, to the president, Dr. Thomas A. Graves, Jr.

Her persistence, aided perhaps by a little luck, won out, and she was admitted to William and Mary. She went to Williamsburg in the fall of 1974 at the age of 18, intending to pursue her studies in Spanish with a view toward teaching, but never forgetting her first love, writing.

As part of her liberal arts program, she began taking courses in theater, including one called "Introduction to Theater," with Dr. Louis Catron, an expert in teaching the art and technique of playwriting. His text is widely used in colleges around the country.

"I remember walking into his office," Karen recalled, "and saying 'I want to be a writer.' And his reply was 'Yes, but do you want to write?' I learned a great deal from Dr. Catron. In addition to the fundamentals of playwriting, he helped me understand that writing takes a lot of discipline and dedication—that it is just hard work."

"Of course, I remember Karen," Catron said. "We have kept in close touch through the years. She first came in as a sophomore, I think, was well dressed, attractive, with a certain air of determination about her. She was a loner, she had her own dreams when she came to college, as we all do. But I think that even then her personal plans and aspirations were high and, in a way, different from those of her classmates and sorority sisters. Most of them were Virginia stereotypes, planning for a home, a family—maybe a job. They wanted to succeed as the everyday housewife. Karen dreamed much bigger. And she was ready to learn how to make the dreams come true. Although she was an independent spirit, with romantic notions about being a writer, she was also willing to learn and to adapt."

During her time at the college her basic attitudes toward writing changed, Catron recalled. "She came to realize how much time she had to spend on her craft. And she also learned to accept criticism gracefully, professionally, not as an attack on her."

Most important of all, perhaps, "She learned that she had to write from inside, from what was in her heart and gut, not to hide anything or copy from others."

At the core of Catron's teaching was his demand that each student develop and perfect his or her personal credo and write from that point of view. "This free association of ideas and values important to their lives helps them establish priorities and get a perspective for their writing," Catron said. In Karen's case, the credo became a big influence in shaping her career.

Hall looks back on Catron and her work in his classes as invaluable for her later development and success. "Without him, without the discipline of those classes, I wouldn't be here in Hollywood today."

"Karen and I learned together, in a sense," Catron said. "I taught her the fundamentals of drama and playwriting,

CHAPTER THREE

but in turn she taught me that television drama was an inherent part of playwriting and not a separate or isolated entity.

"Our work at the college concentrates not only on writing for the stage, but also gets the students involved in production: staging, lighting, directing—all the essential components. And in their involvement they come to understand each component better.

"The production of a play is important to writers," Catron continued, "especially if it's their own play. I understood Karen's search for instant gratification. Shakespeare had this in his time. He saw his plays on the stage almost as soon as he finished writing them, and he could join in the audience appreciation, too."

Writing original one-act plays—three a semester—was one of the challenges of the course, and through competition, the best plays were produced each year in the Premiere Theater at the college. "A one-act play is roughly the equivalent of a half-hour TV show," Karen commented, "and all this writing turned out to be marvelous training. But at some point I had begun to run out of good ideas and wanted to try adapting a story to the *M*A*S*H* format. The trouble was I didn't know exactly what the format should look like. But I found some slightly outdated books in the library and they gave me useful guidelines."

In 1977, during the summer of her junior year in college, Karen had an opportunity to join a short seminar on TV writing being conducted in California by the University of Richmond. The trip came at a bad time for her because her one-act play *Bird Dogs* was going to be produced by a theater group in Chatham. Nevertheless, she couldn't resist the chance to visit Hollywood and see the industry firsthand. TV producer-writer Earl Hamner, with whom she had been corresponding, was an alumnus of the University of Richmond and met with the students when they came to California, took them onto working sets, and generally opened up unparalleled insights into the business. "I particularly remember his comments about *The Waltons* and TV in general," Karen recalled. "He said '*The Waltons* is a top-quality show floating on a sea of garbage.' That may have been prejudiced, but it did stick with me."

During this trip, Karen and the others also visited the *M*A*S*H* set and she was able to get some sample scripts. More important, however, she met Alan Alda. During their talk she told him that she was missing the production of her one-act play in Chatham, and that she had named the lead character after his wife because of their similarities. Alda encouraged her to send him samples of her work when she returned home, and said he would get back to her.

A long-distance correspondence began, extending over more than two years, and culminating with Karen's invitation to meet the *M*A*S*H* producers in 1980 to discuss some of her promising script proposals for possible production. But there were still some unexpected turns and detours on the long, 3,000-mile road from Main Street in Chatham to West Pico Boulevard in Los Angeles.

When she returned to William and Mary after her trip to California, Karen switched to a major in English and moved into the Kappa Delta sorority house. She continued her playwriting courses with renewed vigor and inspiration.

Her dilemma of what to do after graduating from college was solved in the spring of 1978. With Dr. Catron's assistance, she applied for and won a $2,700 fellowship from the Virginia Museum of Fine Arts for graduate study in drama at the University of Virginia. As she finished her undergraduate work and prepared to move to Charlottesville, Karen wrote a thoughtful letter to her parents, the kind many students may compose in their minds but rarely get down on paper. "I know it's been hard putting me through college, and you've made sacrifices. But I want you to know how much I appreciate it. I've done more than become educated; I've also grown up a lot, and being away from home has taught me

CHAPTER THREE

how much you mean to me. I hope you'll always be proud of me and never be disappointed in what I make of my life. I'm very lucky to have had you for parents."

Then Karen added a characteristic afterthought: "Of course, you were lucky to have me." It is this kind of zinger, sometimes sentimental, sometimes cutting, that typifies the dialogue she wrote for *M*A*S*H* and other shows.

The year she spent at the University of Virginia was a lonely one. "In some ways, I think it was a lost year," her father said. "For one thing, the course work and challenges didn't seem to fit Karen's style and needs at the time." There was little interest in TV writing per se. She also was on a tight budget and took two outside jobs, one at McDonald's, to make ends meet. During the preceding summer, she had organized a monster yard-and-garage sale to build her bank account, and according to her mother, "sold about anything around the place that wasn't tied down."

But Karen kept working on her writing and had one play, *Poison Gas*, produced at the university. And she kept writing scripts on "spec" (without a commitment from the producers to use the material) for shows like *Taxi* and *Eight Is Enough*. Toward the end of the year, an encouraging phone call from *Taxi* producer Jim Burrows persuaded her that the time had come to go west.

When she left Charlottesville in 1979, Karen boarded a jet for California with about $1,600 in her pocket, and no specific job prospects in hand. But she was fully determined to beat Earl Hamner's 100-to-1 odds and become a scriptwriter. The local banker in Chatham had refused to lend her any money for the trip, arguing that "there are already lots of would-be writers in Hollywood and they're all broke." But her father cosigned a note, and she flew west. It was typical of Karen that when she finally did sell her first script, the proceeds went immediately back to the banker to repay the loan. As is usually the case, Hollywood did not quite welcome her with open arms, though she did have a couple of valuable aces in the hole, Hamner and Alan Alda. After several fruitless weeks in the city, Karen made an uncharacteristically despondent phone call to home. Flo Hall listened carefully and persuaded her to give it a real try—"stay on a while longer—hang in there." Karen picked up a few temporary jobs doing secretarial work to sustain her (one was with a company called *Ping Pong Productions*), and then got a small toehold doing clerical work and a little writing for commercials Orson Welles was making.

One day in 1980 Alda's secretary called with Alan's request that she send more of her work to the *M*A*S*H* producers because they were looking for a new writer, "preferably a woman." She was asked to come to the studio and "pitch ideas" about possible scripts. "They respected my knowledge of the show," Karen recalled, "and they liked the ideas, too. I got my first chance then to do a script. It was called 'Father's Day,' about a time when Major Houlihan's father visits *M*A*S*H*. They bought the script, and it went on the air December 8, 1980." She was on her way.

"Actually, I became the first and only woman writer on staff," Karen commented, "although Linda Bloodworth and Mary Kay Place had done two scripts together earlier."

After two productive, educational years as writer and executive story editor for *M*A*S*H*, Karen helped plan and write the climactic closing episode of the show. At that point she had already been recruited to write for another top-rated program, *Hill Street Blues*. That show had already received critical and public approval, and Karen welcomed the chance to move into an entirely new situation. For the next couple of years she and the show prospered. She thrived on the new challenges and once wrote about why *Hill Street* succeeded. "[We] created a world full of as many inconsistencies and absurdities as life itself. . . . The characters are not glamorous . . . they look tired; they look like they are working. The cops on the Hill have quick tempers, narrow minds, bad grammar, and a mediocre sense of humor. In short, they are human."

CHAPTER THREE

For her work on *Hill Street* (where she was, again, the only woman staff writer), Karen won the recognition of her peers with two nominations from the Writer's Guild and three Emmy nominations for her scripts, including her own favorite, "Officer of the Year."

During the same period, Karen began writing full-length movies for television production, and in 1985 one of them, *Toughlove*, starring Bruce Dern and Lee Remick, was rated tenth nationally the week it was aired.

In the course of the next 18 months, Karen began doing research and interviews for a two-hour film on the life of former First Lady Betty Ford that the ABC network had commissioned. Before developing the full script, she spent weeks on background, which included visiting the Fords' homes in Aspen and Palm Springs and talking with all of the members of the Ford family. "This was a complex and sensitive story to tell," Karen said, "and it covers major parts of their lives. Through all our visits and discussions, I developed a good rapport and friendship with the Fords."

As soon as Karen had concluded her work on the Ford script, she moved on to a new and difficult assignment as supervising producer for the 1986 surprise hit series *Moonlighting*. She approached this slightly madcap show with characteristic enthusiasm. "I've always loved dialogue, you know. I like to get at the heart of the story and the characters, and dialogue is vital to the nature and moods of *Moonlighting*."

"It's important to understand that Maddie and David, [the show's main characters] have really distinctive rhythms in their speech . . . they have certain words they would or wouldn't use . . . that's the kind of thing that's easy for me to pick up, and it can make or break a script . . . the dialogue has to be fast and glib and yet convincing enough to hold the story together."

In addition to her production responsibilities, Karen also continues to write an occasional script. "That's what I still love best. I hope I can always keep writing," she said.

There is a personal side to Karen's story as well. In June 1983, just after her twenty-seventh birthday, Karen married TV producer Sheldon Bull of Pasadena, whom she met through a mutual friend, their agent. Their wedding was in Arcadia, California, and Karen's half brother, Bryant Wilbourne, performed the ceremony.

The determination to write seems to run in Karen's family. Her younger sister, Barbara, came to work in Hollywood after graduation from James Madison University in 1982. Since then she has emulated the Hall fast track by selling scripts to programs like *Newhart* and *Family Ties*, and to Disney Productions. She's now executive story editor for *Easy Street*, a new ABC program.

Karen tries to return to Virginia with some regularity to visit her family and friends, remembering her roots, savoring the sights and sounds of rural Pittsylvania County, taking an afternoon off to talk with advanced English students in Mrs. Todd's old classroom at the end of the corridor. She answers questions about actors Alda and Mike Farrell, but she spends more time urging them to get ready for the heavy demands of college reading, no matter what their major.

On one of those trips east she and Sheldon visited William and Mary to talk with theater students and aspiring writers, and then have dinner as honored guests in the president's house, a little over 10 years after Karen had written for his support in gaining admission.

Much of the time, however, Karen Hall is hard at work in her second-story office in Hollywood. Just opposite the gates of the studio that houses her office there is a verdant public golf course, with flowering shrubs and acacia trees. Farther along, there are fast-food stores, laundromats, and churches—all the mundane components that make up life on the western spur of Main Street, America, thousands of miles from Chatham.

She's in a creative enclave where she and other writers

CHAPTER THREE

carry out their unique role of shaping and reshaping a fictitious world that must at once reflect, inspire, entertain, and satisfy television's vast and unpredictable audience. There is an ebb and flow between the two worlds, and a kind of continuing transition that Karen Hall has been making most of her life.

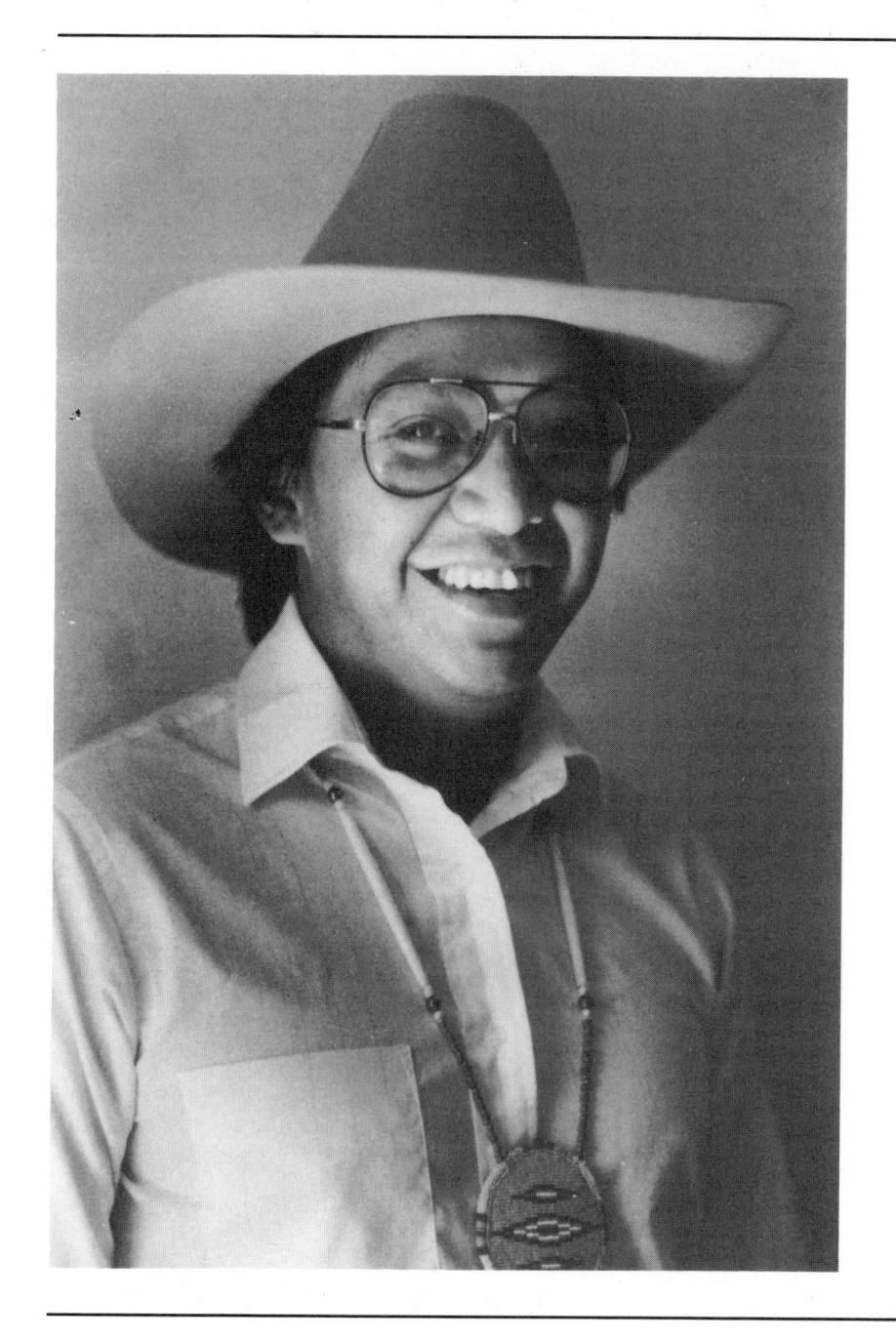

Chapter 4

ANTHONY KAHN

Two generations before Anthony Kahn was born, his grandfather was told by the Bureau of Indian Affairs (BIA) to stop using his traditional Navajo name, which meant "Long Moustache," and to select a new one from an approved list of four- or five-letter surnames chalked on a board in the bureau's office at Window Rock, Arizona.

The conflict between Anthony's two worlds was established even longer ago than that when Europeans on horseback invaded Indian lands in the Southwest. First came the Spanish, looking for cities of gold; then the trappers and traders; and, finally, the armies, the bluecoats of the U.S. Cavalry.

The Navajos and Apaches and Hopis adapted, moved, ran, hid, and fought back. By the late 1860s, the fighting was pretty much over. After defeat and imprisonment, the Navajos were offered a permanent homeland on the barren upland plateaus extending over northwestern New Mexico and northeastern Arizona.

CHAPTER FOUR

Like most of the 200,000 Navajos who today live on or near their vast 32,000-square-mile reservation, Tony, as everyone calls him, continues to face perplexing questions of identity. How can he preserve and protect the best of his Indian heritage and culture and yet share in the opportunities, benefits, and responsibilities of the modern, industrialized country that touches, taxes, surrounds, but somehow never quite absorbs his Navajo nation?

Tony Kahn has faced these questions almost since his birth in 1961 in Gallup, New Mexico, the self-proclaimed "Indian capital of the world." He is a full-blooded Navajo who has lived off and on the reservation and studied in Indian schools and public schools. In the late spring of 1986, he received a B.S. degree in mechanical engineering from Stanford, one of the most selective universities in the country. To achieve this distinction, he defied great statistical odds, becoming one of very few Navajos who complete college. While nearly 80 percent of all Americans now graduate from high school, the completion rate for Navajos is just over 40 percent. About 2,500 Navajos each year go on to colleges and universities, and a similar number enter vocational training programs. Of those who go to college, very few complete a degree, perhaps 2 or 3 percent. Money remains the biggest stumbling block.

Tony Kahn's Stanford experience took him through a demanding and difficult six years of study, work, and time off. Then in the winter of 1987 he started his first full-time job as an engineer with the Arizona Public Service Company and was assigned to the giant Four Corners power plant about six miles east of Fruitland, New Mexico, on the border of the reservation. He is part of a team directly responsible for the operating efficiency and maintenance of three major generating units at the plant.

On a cold, sunny day in late February, he stood outside the huge facility and talked about his schooling, his hopes, and his aspirations. He was dressed in a windbreaker, plaid shirt, jeans, and work boots, and sported tinted, aviator-style glasses with dark rims; his thick black hair was cut moderately full and parted in the middle. He spoke with the accent of the Western plains, often mixing engineering terms with campus slang and references to sports and TV shows.

"We really have two kinds of Navajos now," he said. "The traditional ones who grow up speaking only the Navajo language, send their kids to Bureau of Indian Affairs schools nearby, and tend to remain on the reservation to farm or maybe work. Then there's the other kind that I guess I represent, who are brought up to be bilingual and who go to school in more urban situations, bigger towns like Chinle or Window Rock, and feel strongly motivated to go outside, to move on—get jobs, get married, buy four-wheel drives, the whole nine yards." He paused. "A few even go on to college, but that's very tough even now, and not many do it. Only a small percentage of those who do go to college ever finish their degrees. I was lucky. I stuck with it, and my family was always behind me."

As Tony began an informal walking tour of the plant, he talked with pride and confidence about the challenges of his new job, and its place in the conflict of his two worlds. "The original plant here was built about 25 years ago, and it's been one of the biggest in the whole Southwest, I guess. Recently, they have added new capacity, more powerful and efficient units, over there." He pointed at the larger chimneys to the east.

A muffled but intense combination of sounds from the furnaces and turbines permeated the desert air. There was a feeling of raw energy and carefully controlled power everywhere. Five immense concrete chimneys, each over 10 stories high, dominated the local landscape, and their billowing plumes of almost pure steam could be seen for 20 miles in any direction. From the Navajo Coal Company just next door, conveyors endlessly scooped black anthracite from great conical mounds and moved it toward the furnaces.

CHAPTER FOUR

After a quick ride up in a wire-cage elevator, Tony stood on a narrow wooden platform near the top of the plant and looked west across the snow-covered plateau toward an imposing monolith that was clearly visible some 15 miles away, an immobile red stone ship rising 1,400 feet above the plain. "That's Shiprock," he said. "It's been on a lot of TV commercials and calendars, I guess. The town is a bit farther to the north. And those peaks way out there are in southern Colorado." Distances shrink in the crystalline desert air; mountains 40 miles away appear to be almost within walking distance.

"Our family home is at Lukachukai, in Arizona, beyond that range," he said, gesturing toward the west and south. "Those are the Chuska Mountains. But it's nearly 150 miles by road. About a two-hour drive around here." He was not exaggerating. Cars and trucks often seem to ignore the posted 55-miles-per-hour speed limit.

From the platform, it was easy to trace the parade of thick cables and supporting towers that stretched into the distance, carrying 500-kilovolt lines and running hundreds of miles through the Southwest, bringing power to the casinos at Las Vegas, to the businesses, homes, and country clubs outside Phoenix, and to the sound stages and TV studios in Hollywood. Few serve the adjacent Navajo reservation where an estimated 75 percent of the homes have no electricity; many are still lit by gas lantern, and the great majority still have no running water. Some members of Tony's family must travel seven miles for cooking and drinking water.

"But those things are changing," Tony said. "Electricity alone won't solve all our problems; it's a lot more complicated. Many people prefer to live the way they have for a long time, independent or maybe dependent on nature, what they grow and produce themselves." Despite the drastic livestock reduction programs in the 1940s and 1950s, about a third of the Navajos on the reservation today make a living raising goats, horses, sheep, and cattle. Many lead seminomadic lives, in tune with nature, moving with the changing seasons from the sheltered valleys in winter to the high plateaus in summer.

"The adjustment is hard for a lot of people; some never make it," he continued. "We are getting more people through school all the time now. That's what we need, more educated people at home, and technical people who know what they're talking about. That's one reason I studied to become an engineer."

Tony's words recall those of an earlier tribal leader, Sam Ahkeah, who during the 1950s urged young Navajos to go into education. "You are our future," he told them. "We need thousands of young lawyers, doctors, nurses, accountants, engineers, business students. We don't want them to get an education and take jobs off the reservation. We need them here!"

"That is the problem," Tony said. "We need more young people involved, on the reservation and off. We need to develop what we have, but also to build bridges to the outside."

Tony Kahn reflected on the course of a tribal leader he knows better, Peter MacDonald, who has served three terms as elected council chairman. MacDonald's life has cut across a segment of time during which the Navajos have made important strides into the modern world, and he has been a symbolic force for both the old and the new.

MacDonald was born on the reservation in a small village near the Four Corners intersection, learned Navajo as a first language, and went through local schools. At 16, however, he went outside, enlisted in the Marines during World War II, and served as one of about 400 Navajo "codetalkers," who distinguished themselves in the Pacific theater by devising a complex secret code from their own language that the Japanese could not decipher.

After the war, MacDonald finished high school and junior college with honors and received a B.S. degree in electrical engineering at the University of Oklahoma. He worked as an

CHAPTER FOUR

engineer in southern California for several years, but returned to the Navajo reservation in the 1960s, immersed himself in tribal government, and won the position of tribal chairman first in 1970.

The lessons of MacDonald's life and leadership were not lost on Tony Kahn. "There are many different ways to have an impact," he said. "I think we are learning how to draw the best from both worlds and use it to our advantage."

Stanford's assistant dean for student affairs, James Larimore, watched Tony's leadership abilities develop at the university. "He assimilated a Stanford education without sacrificing any of his heritage, and without having his own personality changed. He was involved in a lot of activities on campus, and he always seemed to be named chairman. He has that special ability to formulate ideas, organize groups, focus on basic goals."

Tony grew up feeling the strong pull of his Navajo roots, but steadily absorbing the realities of the outside world. He has lived in one-room family hogans with dirt floors and smoke holes in the roofs. But he has also lived in the modern dormitories at Stanford and seen the parking areas sprinkled with BMWs, owned by students fully prepared to pay the $17,000 a year it costs to attend the university. His own tribal scholarship, matched in part by Stanford, seemed frail currency amid the opulence on campus. Tony had to find several part-time jobs while he was there to help pay his way—he cut lawns, painted houses, and tutored freshmen at the intercultural center.

As he continued to walk through the power plant, past an intricate maze of gleaming steam pipes, massive electrical conduits, and whirring generators, Tony reflected on recent national studies by the Department of the Interior that tell of the worsening conditions on Indian reservations around the country. A 1986 study found that 41 percent of all reservation Indians were living below the poverty level, compared to 12 percent of the total U.S. population, and that well over half of all Navajo males between the ages of 20 and 64 were unemployed, against 12 percent of all Americans.

Yet, the Peabody Coal Company, the largest in the United States, is located on Navajo land, and at least half of all the government's uranium reserves are there, plus an estimated 100 million barrels of oil. Unfortunately, uranium royalties have been decreasing steadily in the 1980s, and oil and coal income is also way down. Further, the Navajos receive only about 4 percent of the value of the coal mined and 3 percent of the uranium.

One tribal leader recently summed up the inequity in everyday terms: "The tribe gets 29 cents a ton average for coal and pays 45 cents a can for Coca Cola."

"Sure, we have plenty of problems to solve on the reservation," Tony agreed, "and in our relationship with the government. In the last five years or so we have lost about 30 percent of our federal funds through budget cuts. That's $150 million. A lot of jobs were lost, too. There's big unemployment on the reservation, I'd say close to 60 percent today. And another thing is that the pay here is not comparable to that for most outside jobs." Of the 20,000 Navajos who do work on the reservation, about two-thirds are in public health, education, and government jobs, mainly in Window Rock, Shiprock, and Tuba City.

Even by optimistic estimates, the mineral riches will not last forever. "I doubt that our known reserves will last much beyond the end of the century," Tony said. "Somehow we have to develop alternate sources of energy on the reservation—solar, wind, whatever."

After he finished work that day, Tony continued the discussion over dinner in Farmington. He looked back at his early education and talked about his parents' background. He had just made arrangements to rent a house nearby that would give him a base, only a short commuting distance from work, and also provide space for family members on their visits to the area. The ties between Tony, his sisters,

CHAPTER FOUR

and their children remain close and cordial; the Kahn family continues a long-standing tradition of sharing home, food, and resources.

"My folks traveled around a lot when we were young," Tony reported. "Not because they necessarily wanted to—they went where the jobs were. My father was an artist and craftsman, he learned silversmithing and also did a lot of painting and illustrating. He did two books that I know of. I remember when I was just a kid, watching him work, and trying to sketch myself . . . he would show me steps for loosening up, practice drills, things like that."

Art is still a serious pastime for Tony, and he might well make a living at it if he ever decided to leave engineering. On the wall of Stanford's intercultural center there is a bright and fanciful life-sized mural that he painted as an undergraduate. His oil and acrylic paintings of Navajo scenes, life and history, have also been exhibited elsewhere on campus, and he won special acclaim for a bronze replica of the Great Seal of the Navajo tribe, with its representation of the four magic mountains, the blessings of nature, and encircling broken rainbow and border of arrowheads.

His parents come from large families that still live in the area. Some of his uncles run livestock outside Lukachukai. His father, Chester Kahn, was born in Pine Springs, Arizona, and grew up there. His mother was born in a hogan in Lukachukai, not many miles from where she lives today.

"But when both of them were about high school age, they were sent away to boarding school, and that's where they met," Tony said, "in Stewart, Nevada, a small place near Carson City. The BIA policy in those days was pretty much the same as it had been for a hundred years—they felt the kids should leave home and be sent away to 'proper' schools. That's exactly the opposite of traditional Navajo beliefs, which stress close home and family ties. But as I said, these things have all been changing with the times, and most of the good schools were, in fact, away from the reservation. So they met there, in Stewart, and after finishing high school, they were married."

Tony's mother, Annie Kahn, has her own, generally negative view of her early teachers and the BIA tradition. She recalled with some bitterness that she got little schooling of any kind herself until she was about 12, and no opportunity to learn English. She remembered teachers who were "very tough" on Navajos. "They punished us for speaking Navajo instead of English. It was difficult for me in the early days. Why were we forced to learn English when few or none of the teachers or others made any effort to learn Navajo? Why was the burden to be bilingual on *us*?"

Tony continued his own recollections. "My father worked in the Stewart area. Jobs were hard to find in the 1950s. They lived near Carson City, Nevada, and that's where my first three sisters were born. A bit later, my father had a job as a commercial artist in Flagstaff, and the girls went to school there for a while. My impressionable years were spent there. That's where I learned English, as a first language really, though I did pick up some Navajo, too. My own real schooling began in Gallup, and then we moved to Chinle, on the reservation. My father had a good job with the Office of Navajo Economic Opportunity—some people called it ONEO or, only half joking, 'Only Navajos Eat Onions.' Anyway, he did some fund-raising and traveled to Phoenix and Washington, D.C., and was very active in Indian affairs.

"We all moved through schools in the Chinle area, and I had good examples set for me by my sisters [Nesbah, Charlotte, Marianna, Norma, and Gloria]. They were all excellent students and into all kinds of things.... They won national honor society awards, they were cheerleaders. One [Marianna] went on to college [Fort Lewis College in Durango, Colorado] and then to law school at the University of California at Berkeley. Later, she worked as a lawyer in Flagstaff until she was married. She lives over in Red Mesa now with her husband and children."

CHAPTER FOUR

The next day, Saturday, Tony planned to visit the family compound in Lukachukai for a joint birthday celebration for two of his sisters' children. The drive from Farmington is about 150 miles across the high, barren plateau. The vast Navajo reservation covers a territory the size of the entire state of West Virginia. There are no fences or markers of any kind to indicate where state property ends and the reservation begins.

During the trip, Tony talked about the next stages of his education. On the western edge of Farmington, he pointed out the Navajo Mission Academy where he completed most of his high school education. "My folks had always made education a priority for us," he said. "Whenever they made a job change or moved, they always tried to make sure we would get into a good school. As I got closer to high school age, my mother was looking around, talking to people about the best place to go that would lead to college. She had heard about the mission school here and we all talked it over at home.

"For me, it meant leaving a lot of my friends and being away most of the year. And it meant sacrifices for the family, too. It seemed really expensive then, maybe $300 a year. But they said they could handle it if I wanted to go. I said, 'Why not give it a shot?'

"I thought it would be tough, and it was. Everyone at the school had to do physical labor. In addition to class work we mowed lawns, washed dishes, helped clean the place up. But we got off a lot of weekends so we could go home, and that made the transition a little easier."

Begun in 1976 on a small scale, the Mission Academy is run essentially by the United Methodist Church and has grown into a cluster of handsome brick-and-wood classroom buildings, dormitories, a library and chapel, and athletic fields. After an initial enrollment of only about a dozen students, the school had expanded to about 100 by the time

Tony attended and now has over 200 students, almost all of whom are college-bound. It is characterized as the only college preparatory school for American Indians in the United States, and its mandate is "to provide Navajo youth the necessary education to enable them to succeed in the academic and professional worlds so they may return to become future leaders of the Navajo nation."

Its headmaster, Dillon Platero, was for many years a leader in the advancement of Navajo education on the reservation. He once summed up his philosophy: "Self-sufficiency is as vital to an institution as it is to the individual. . . . The academy strives for self-sufficiency, building on a history of self-determination and tribal commitment to ensure the continued quality of education for gifted students of the Navajo nation."

"We weren't aware of heavy goals like that in those days," Tony said. "It was a pretty small place. But I knew it was a real opportunity for me and I worked hard at it. We lived in supervised dorms, each with a counselor. We had a fairly rigid schedule: early breakfast, work, and then classes, starting at 8:30 a.m. and running until lunch. Then more classes until about 3 p.m. or so, when we were free for study, sports, whatever, until the evening study hours.

"We had a solid college-prep curriculum," Tony recalled. "I took 4½ years of math along with English, social studies, and science. We worked hard, and the teachers were sharp, and we had small classes with a lot of personal attention. I especially remember my math teacher, Bill Floor. He was a real sports enthusiast and drew lots of parallels between sports and learning; he made it interesting and exciting, and he encouraged us all to go on to school, go as far as we could.

"I got into sports on a recreational basis and I still enjoy playing basketball. The academy does pretty well now in competition with other area schools in several sports—they have had some top teams in basketball lately, and wrestling,

CHAPTER FOUR

too. [The Eagles football team made the New Mexico state playoffs for the first time in 1986, and one of its wrestlers was the 105-pound AAA state champion.]

"We had a small graduating class in my time," Tony noted. "We all went on to college, though. I started looking at places like the University of New Mexico and Arizona State. I was a big football fan of theirs. I also considered Berkeley, because my sister had been there. I read catalogs and college handbooks, and we had a counselor at the academy who helped me out."

The idea of also applying to Stanford came largely by chance. "I really didn't know much about the place," Tony recalled. "I had never talked to anyone from there. I had never been on the campus. But I did know about Jim Plunkett. I knew he had helped Stanford's football team win the Rose Bowl, and that wasn't bad. [Plunkett, now an aging NFL quarterback with the L.A. Raiders, has Indian ancestry.]

"Later, I learned that Stanford had a great engineering school and that it was in a good climate, so I decided to apply there, too. Eventually, it became my first choice. I had no idea of my chances of getting in or how tough the competition would be.

"I took the SAT exams, filled out all the applications, wrote my essay—the whole drill—then I sat back and waited. I thought I had done pretty well: I had good grades and I was in the ninetieth percentile on the SAT math section. But in English I was in only about the seventy-fifth percentile. I wasn't that great in English." He modestly didn't mention that he was named student of the year at the academy.

In the spring of 1979, with most of the family gathered around at Lukachukai, the letter came. "I guess it was the most exciting day of my life. We had all been waiting and watching; we were on pins and needles. I saw the envelope, and I felt good. It was a thick one. I knew that was a good sign. I ripped it open. The first thing it said was something like 'Congratulations!' I didn't read much more after that. I was jumping all over the place. I was ecstatic. It wasn't until later that I began worrying about how to pay my way, and how it would be to leave home, pretty much for good—to take that big first step into a world I knew very little about."

Tony paused in his recollection and concentrated on driving. New Mexico's Route 504 is a two-lane blacktop highway that unrolls due west from Farmington through the small town of Shiprock, and crosses the state line into Arizona, where it becomes Route 160. The road passes Peter MacDonald's birthplace, Teec Nos Pos, and goes on to Mexican Water, the turn-off for Round Rock and Lukachukai. The land is isolated and deserted, covered by a low growth of juniper and mesquite bushes. A coating of light snow accentuated the subtle shadings of red that touched the fantastic rock shapes along the route. An occasional group of sheep or cattle grazed in the distance, and to the right loomed the high mountains of southern Utah, clearly etched against the deep blue sky but easily 40 miles away.

There is beauty and loneliness in the landscape. Small villages and trading posts (country stores, really, with gas pumps and sometimes a snack bar) are often 50 miles apart. It's no place for a car to break down, and one is tempted to agree with Daniel Webster, who once described the Arizona territory as "a barren waste of prairie dogs, cactus, and shifting sands, incapable of producing anything and therefore not worth retaining." Of course, he could not have known then what riches lay beneath the inhospitable rocks.

Tony pointed out a small cluster of wood-frame buildings, mobile homes, forlorn bleachers, and a football field that nestled in the shelter of an impressive mesa. "That's Red Mesa," he noted, "the place I mentioned where my sister lives with her family. Her husband teaches social science in the school. She's pretty much a full-time mother now. I don't know when she might get back to the law again. They'll be at the house for lunch."

It is still another 50 or 60 miles to the Lukachukai area,

CHAPTER FOUR

through gently rolling valleys and ridges. There was almost no traffic in either direction. Much of the area is about a mile above sea level, but peaks of the Chuska Mountains to the east reach 9,000 feet and were coated with recent snow.

Everywhere there are exquisite land forms, solitary pillars and buttes of red sandstone, rounded knobs and sharp upthrusts carved and shaped by wind and water. Few living things moved across the gray-green brush cover. The silence was intense; not even the cry of a bird disturbed the tranquillity.

Outside the settlement of Lukachukai itself, Tony turned off onto a rutted dirt road that winds several hundred yards down to a small cluster of frame houses and hogans that represent his family home.

Lunch would be served inside the hogan that he had been using, one that he helped build and decorate. This typical Navajo dwelling had one room of rough plaster over a wood frame, roughly octagonal in shape, with a green asphalt shingle roof and a single hole for a metal stovepipe.

Inside there was the pleasant odor of wood burning in the stove. The floor was red dirt and the place was simply furnished with a makeshift clothes rack, a child's crib, a trestle table, and some chairs. On the walls were posters and calendars from the Stanford years, and several of Tony's paintings. There was a sign advertising the Eleventh Annual Powwow that he helped plan and run in May 1982. Assorted college texts stood on a wooden shelf. Out back a few yards was a basic wooden privy, and on the level portion of the driveway, a basketball backboard with a rusted hoop.

Tony's mother and one sister live in an adjacent wood-frame house from which a TV antenna rises, and near it there is a low, earth-covered mound that serves as a sweat house, the Navajo equivalent of a sauna.

Soon, Tony's mother and oldest sister, Nesbah, arrived carrying a large covered aluminum cooking pot and a few paper bags full of apples and rolls. As they made preparations for lunch, Annie Kahn talked about Tony. "He was our only son, the youngest born, so he never had to wear the hand-me-downs for clothes that his sisters did. He didn't go to kindergarten—there wasn't any. But we had community-organized early education classes, so he learned reading—English first, Navajo later."

Annie Kahn is a young-looking grandmother, with a durable quality about her and a certain grace. She has smooth bronze skin. Her eyes are dark and warm, but when she touched on certain topics, like the BIA, there was a spark of hostility and determination in them, too. She was wearing a loose-fitting blue velour dress highlighted by handsome strands of turquoise beads and a wide hammered-silver bracelet. Her dark hair shows only a few streaks of gray, though she has raised five daughters and a son under a variety of conditions and today lives in a modest home off the paved road, seven miles from water, with intermittent electricity and no plumbing. She has lived in the cities, but she's comfortable here, even serene. She is at once the traditional Navajo and a modern mother who sought the best for her children.

"We knew that a good education was the only path for them," she said. "We didn't have many books around, a few magazines, usually no TV. They could go to the libraries when we lived in Flagstaff and in Chinle, though the one in Chinle was much smaller. But we knew they had to find ways to grow and still keep their own culture. It's important to know yourself, who you are, to understand your own needs and to preserve your identity. You must have those inner resources to call on, wherever you go, no matter what you do—your own storehouse. The family must be a part of all this, to give you strength and meaning." She paused and put her arm around Tony. "I'm really proud of my son and what he has accomplished. What he's doing is important—for us and for him. He's trying to balance family, tribe, culture, and profession. It's not easy to do."

CHAPTER FOUR

Her observations were interrupted as the others arrived for lunch. Two more daughters came in with their children who were all decked out in brightly colored homemade cotton dresses and eager for the party to begin. Lunch was served informally at a wooden table covered with oilcloth. Lamb stew was the main dish, mixed with pungent, homegrown corn, and it was ladled from the large cooking pot into plain white china bowls. There were rolls, apples, and coffee to go around—the basic ingredients of a good Navajo meal.

The young people moved on to their aunt's home down the road for cake and the birthday celebration. Annie Kahn continued to talk about Tony. She spoke well, almost colloquially, though she did not learn much English until her early teens. She had been to Stanford a couple of times, including Tony's graduation, and she was keenly aware of his conflicts, of his opportunities beyond the reservation. Yet she knew the need for educated leaders to remain at home and help the Dine', the Navajo people.

"Tony will develop a meaning to his life, his own special purpose," she said. "He will make his own decisions and find a way to set his goals, based on his personal convictions and origins."

Later in the day, Tony's mother joined him on the drive farther south to visit the Canyon de Chelly, a deep gorge carved into layers of red sandstone. Only a trickle of water along the sandy bottom land traces the course of the river that twists some 30 miles through the heart of the reservation. The canyon is at once a national monument and tourist center; and for the Navajos, a holy place and one of sad memories, too.

As they stood at the overlook, Tony talked about the time over a hundred years ago when his ancestors surrendered to Colonel Kit Carson, and of the "Long Walk" of some 300 miles by thousands of Navajos across the Continental Divide to their imprisonment in the infamous Bosque Redondo near Fort Sumner, New Mexico.

"I guess the only good thing that came out of that was the treaty of 1868, which established the reservation and enabled the people to return there," he said. "The government promised that it would provide a competent elementary school teacher for every 30 Navajo children, and we agreed to make all the children, boys and girls, between the ages of 6 and 16, attend school."

It took a long time to work all that out. It wasn't until the end of the nineteenth century that missionary teachers were replaced by government employees. There were gains and losses on both sides; failures, inconsistencies, misunderstandings, and distrust.

Inevitably, the upheaval of World War II had a far-reaching effect on the Navajos and helped bring the tribe closer to its surrounding world. During the 1960s, with the discovery of new mineral resources, better tribal government and organization, and schools, they began edging toward becoming a modern society and having a viable economy. But even by the 1980s there was still only one postsecondary institution (Navajo Community College) on the reservation, and only a few banks despite the considerable accumulation of tribal wealth.

As Tony looked out over the vast canyon where the slanting sun highlighted myriad shades and tones on the reddish walls, he continued his reflections on the past and the present.

"It's not visible from here," he said, "but downstream a mile or so is where our ancestors, the Anasazi, carved the famous White House out of the sheer cliffs—they built some of the first high-rise apartments." He smiled. "And they vanished at some point; no one knows why, or where they went."

Soon his thoughts turned to his own travels, less than 10 years ago, when he first packed his few belongings and

CHAPTER FOUR

headed west for Stanford. "I knew that going away to college would be the most important turning point in my life," Tony said. "My family put me on the train at the Santa Fe station in Gallup one day in early September. It turned out to be a pretty long and lonely ride. I almost felt like I was in a time capsule or something, being carried from one civilization to another. In a way, I guess I was."

The trip took him nearly two days, across the Western deserts and up the long, fertile valleys of central California. "I got one good break, though," Tony remembered. "I had an aunt who lived in San Jose, so I got off there and had a little time to adjust before I hit the campus." It is hard to overestimate the impact of Stanford University on a solitary 18-year-old Navajo who carried most of his worldly goods onto the campus with him.

The old, original campus remains central, reflecting the California mission style with its pale sandstone buildings and red tile roofs, spacious quadrangles, cool, shaded arcades, neatly trimmed lawns, and graceful palms. But the university has now spread out to all points of the compass. To the north and south lie the new high-tech labs and classrooms, and the world-class medical school. To the west, the linear accelerator is buried in the tawny rolling hills. To the east the old highway, El Camino Real, provides a buffer zone between the school and the prosperous shopping malls and affluent residential areas of Palo Alto. At one edge of the extensive athletic fields stands the 90,000-seat football stadium where a recent NFL Super Bowl was played.

Prosperity and a sense of well-being are everywhere. Among teachers, there are Nobel Prize–winners; among students, Rhodes scholars. The undergraduates have been selected from among the top achievers in high schools around the country. John McEnroe went there, and so did Sally Ride, the first woman in space.

The university is rich; rich in tradition, land, resources, and faculty—everything that counts in a major university. It has recently embarked on a $1 billion fund-raising campaign to mark its one-hundredth anniversary. The only apparent problem today is parking space, which is generally unavailable.

"Talk about culture shock," Tony said. "Everything was totally different for me. Thinking, word patterns, ideas, expectations. Clothes weren't too much of a problem. Blue jeans and a plaid shirt will take you anywhere. But when I first walked into my room at Roble Hall I wasn't sure I would make it. We had about 6 Indians out of 200 in the whole dorm, and just 2 Navajos.

"But I survived those first days. I lived at Roble the first three years." Stanford today has only about 50 Indians of some 15,000 undergraduates; they tend to be about evenly divided between men and women, and many come on tribal scholarships, as Tony did. Although he had the scholarship to start off along with some matching money from Stanford, it still wasn't enough, and during his years at the university Tony worked at part-time jobs to make ends meet.

"It is a small Indian community at Stanford," he said. "But they are diverse, they come from all around the country. That's why the Indian center is important; it helps those who come right off the reservation to understand what's going on, and gives them a touch of home, a chance to relate to something familiar."

The American Indian Cultural Center occupies a series of ground-floor rooms near the main campus and the old Student Union building. Tony's mural of life on the mesa still occupies a place of honor on the wall, and there is comfortable furniture and a welcome feeling of informality in the place.

"I got myself into a lot of activities to make the Indian presence known on campus," Tony recalled. "Once I felt I could deal with the academic demands, I began to explore other things about Stanford. I worked as a program assistant at Roble and as a resident assistant at Robinson House. I did

CHAPTER FOUR

some tutoring at the center. I even taught a class in the Navajo language at one point."

As he moved ahead in his engineering studies, Tony became involved in the Stanford chapter of the American Indian Science and Engineering Society (AISES) and served one year as president. For recreation, he organized an all-Indian basketball team and a tournament at Maples Pavilion. "I don't think the level of play had the NCAA worried," Tony laughed, "but we enjoyed playing and the people around the area learned a little more about Indians."

On two different occasions Tony served as major coordinator for an annual powwow at the university that attracts thousands of visitors each year. While organizing the event, which features exhibitions and demonstrations of Indian culture and history, art and song, he met Carol Webb from nearby San Mateo, and she brought a new dimension into his life.

"She was an expert on Indian social and cultural issues," he said. "We became pretty good friends—close friends. She is half Nez Percé and her mother is a full-blooded Nez Percé."

Carol is also very attractive and her portrait in full Indian regalia has appeared on Bay Area cultural calendars. Tony confided that their friendship and her deep involvement in Indian affairs accentuated and complicated his search for ways to resolve his personal and professional dilemmas.

Two valued mementos from Carol still hang on the rearview mirror of Tony's car. One is a beaded red heart—self-explanatory. The other is a rare white eagle feather from the war bonnet of Carol's grandfather, who served with Chief Joseph during his proud effort to lead his Nez Percé people to sanctuary in Canada.

Toward the end of his third year at Stanford, Tony began to sense he needed time to reconsider his goals and purposes in life. "I was tired of the California lifestyle," he said. "My grandparents were ill, and I knew I needed to spend time with my family."

Jim Larimore, assistant dean at Stanford, recalled the decision. "He needed time to recalibrate his goals, to get a new perspective on his experiences at Stanford. Stopping out is nothing unusual at the university. It's accepted here. I would say nearly one-fourth of all our undergraduates take some time off, finish in five years instead of four."

"I decided to go home for a while—maybe a year," Tony said. "I wanted to reacquaint myself with the Navajo way of life, see friends and relatives, polish my language skills. I felt I was losing a sense of my roots.

"I did spend time with my grandparents before they died. It was a good thing to do. I got into some special ceremonies and learned old Navajo songs and legends from them."

During the year off, he also took a job on the engineering staff at the San Juan power plant outside Farmington, and was the only Navajo employed there in that capacity at the time. "It was a valuable apprenticeship. I could put a lot of my theory from Stanford to work and learn practical aspects of the job there. It was a good deal for me, and not bad for them, either. I was paid only about half as much as the regular engineers.

"Being home solved some things for me, but it made others more difficult. I had a hard time when I returned to Stanford to finish my degree."

One of his advisers in the engineering department, assistant dean Linda Bradford Wells, agreed. "He had a rough time of it," she recalled. "But he made it. I think that being involved in a lot of activities on campus helped him in a way. He learned to adapt but he was able to retain his own personality. He is one of the few Indians that I have met who was really Indian-like—I think he wore a ponytail at some point. He was upwardly mobile and had a lot of leadership qualities. I remember he didn't like the idea of taking a loan to help pay off his indebtedness, so he got a job to pay it off in addition to all his other commitments."

"I was off the track," Tony said. "I didn't take all of my

CHAPTER FOUR

classes seriously. I even failed a couple, so it took me over two years to finish, when I did return. But I finished in good shape. I was happy to hack my way through."

When he graduated in mid-June 1986, his family traveled to the commencement ceremonies on campus and watched with pride. Tony starred in one segment of a fund-raising film about Stanford students, and the alumni newspaper wrote a feature on his achievements at the university.

He began to sort out his options that summer. He stayed in the San Francisco Bay Area for a few weeks, going on job interviews with various companies, and he visited regularly with Carol Webb and her family. He also began to explore the possibility of an engineering job in New Mexico or Arizona.

Early in 1987 Tony found temporary living quarters near Shiprock and began his new job as a mechanical engineer with Arizona Public Service. He is one of about a thousand people in the total work force there, and was assigned to the betterment engineering section for three major elements of the plant. Within a few weeks, he had become deeply involved in the complex and demanding tasks of helping oversee the maintenance and efficiency of his units. His closest co-worker in the section is Tokyo-born Jun Tsukii, an engineer who also went to school in California.

Tony conducts test projects, works occasionally in the computer room, and reads actively to keep up on technical literature and operational practices. His days run from 7:30 a.m. to 4 p.m., with a break for lunch. Although there is a cafeteria, many people, including Tony, tend to bring their own brown-bag lunches.

"My Stanford training was excellent preparation for this job," Tony said. "Both the basic background and the lab work helped. My year over at the San Juan plant also gave me terrific on-the-job experience. It's essentially the same kind of operation over there."

As he left the Canyon de Chelly and drove north across

the barren countryside, Tony Kahn concluded his reminiscences about his life thus far. He remains keenly aware of the challenges and conflicts that face him at age 26. But he also feels the optimism and confidence that have guided him through a remarkable high school and college career and carried him into the first stages of a highly responsible engineering job.

"Where do I go from here?" Tony pondered his own question. "My mother says I have only come halfway home. She says I'm still in a border town now. In her mind, I'm in a twilight zone, I guess. I have made one commitment, but I haven't given up on my people either.

"You know, I might still go into teaching at some point. Maybe here on the reservation. It might work out. The Navajos are the largest and wealthiest tribe in the country. We'll probably be 300,000 strong by the turn of the century. Somehow we need to understand ourselves better, make better use of our physical and cultural resources, our spiritual strengths. We need to learn how to work in greater harmony with the outside world whether we like it or not.

"As a tribe, we have faced a lot of tough choices since the time of the 'Long Walk' to Fort Sumner and the prison camp at Bosque Redondo. We'll have some more difficult decisions to make, and maybe it's part of my mission to be involved in them."

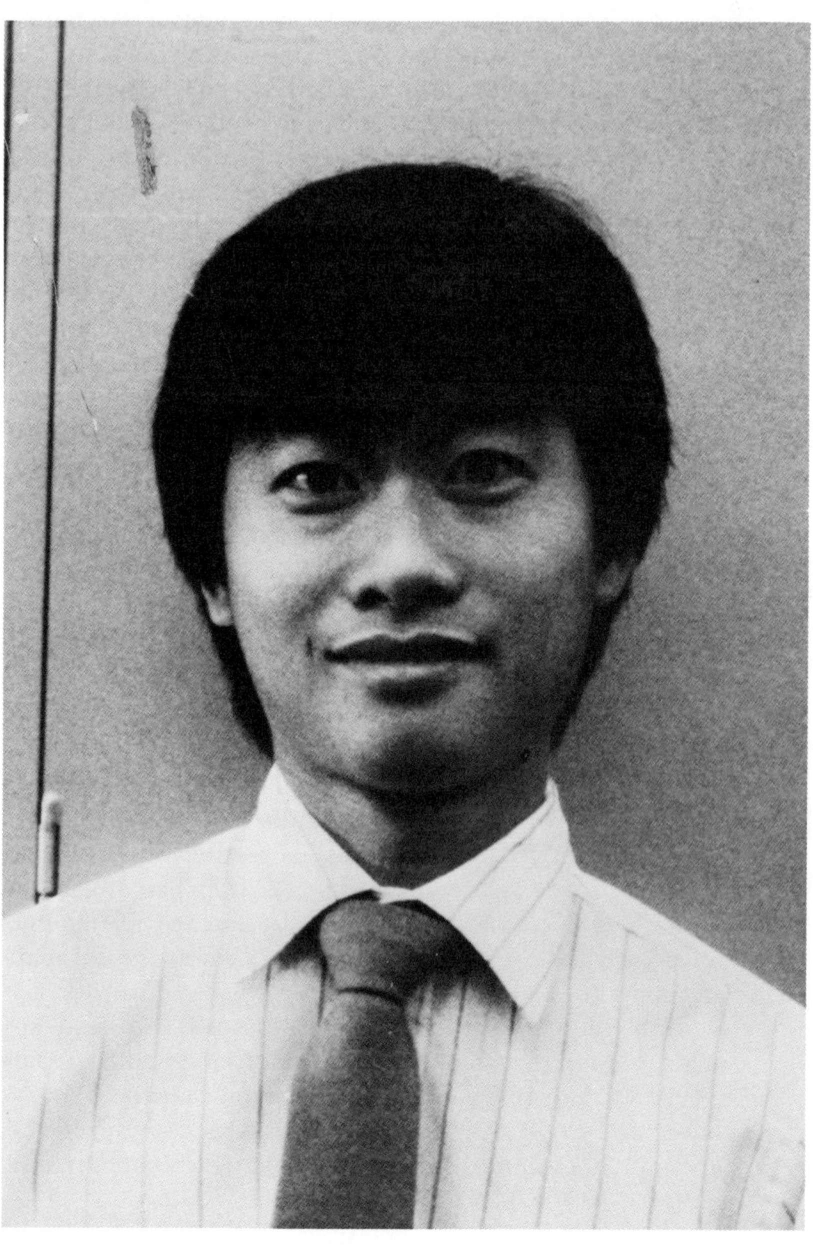

Chapter 5

WINSTON HONG LIEU

If he had waited on you at the Feather 'N Fin take-out store in Norfolk, Virginia, a couple of years ago, you would never have given the slender, brown-skinned boy in the crisp white shirt and jaunty cap a second glance, except to notice that he was efficient, polite, and had a bit of an accent.

What you would never have guessed was that Winston Hong Lieu was in the middle of his regular 5 p.m.-to-midnight shift at the fast-food place, and that he had already put in a full day of classes and engineering labs at Old Dominion University, and a couple of hours working at the computer terminal and reading in the library.

"But I don't study all the time," Winston said, reflecting on his years in the United States since fleeing South Vietnam in 1978. "I find time for other things, too," he added, "music, basketball, you know. . . ." He was wearing a light blue Old Dominion University sweatshirt, faded jeans, and running shoes.

Winston is a wiry 5'7" and might weigh 125 pounds after

CHAPTER FIVE

a heavy dinner. He has dark brown hair and luminous brown eyes, a bright, quick smile, and speaks fluent English overlaid with colloquialisms learned at Feather 'N Fin, from Norfolk area disk jockeys, and from his schoolmates at Granby High School and ODU. Despite Winston's relaxed and informal manner, he has achieved remarkable personal and academic success since coming to the United States as an undersized "orphan" who spoke only a few words and phrases of English gleaned from studying a dictionary in a Malaysian refugee camp.

In December 1985, Winston capped his academic career to date by graduating first in his class of 600 at Old Dominion with a degree in electrical engineering. He completed 151 credit hours in 3½ years in order to move on more quickly to a full-time job with AT&T's Bell Laboratories in New Jersey. His only B (which kept him from a perfect grade-point average) remains a "slight disappointment" to him.

Education and hard work were inseparable for the Lieu family. Winston's father, Thuong Lieu, was a teacher of reading and literature at a private elementary school in Saigon, and his mother, Man Trinh, a seamstress. "My two brothers [Vi and Le] and I have always been taught to do the best you can, try to do your very best, always work hard. There's no limit to what you can do if you have confidence in your abilities," Winston said.

As he looked back, Winston didn't regard his experiences as particularly unusual or exceptional, but rather something that he and his family knew would happen—somehow—if they kept up their faith and determination, and he tends to gloss over the hardships, the dangers, the uncertainties, and especially the loneliness of escaping Vietnam and coming into the strange new land of America.

Winston talked easily about his turbulent past as a teenager in war-torn Saigon ("We didn't actually see that much of the GIs . . . most of the fighting was outside town") and about how enthusiastic he was about starting elementary school where his father was a teacher ("Education came first for all of us . . . it was the most important thing"). He remembered the problems and tensions when the Communists came in, and how the schools had to change in those days. But most of all he remembered the anxious, perilous days and nights of his escape by boat.

"We knew by 1976 when the North Vietnamese Communists began to move into the south that there was not much hope for our family," Winston said. "We knew there was little future for us, and we agreed that we must start . . . planning how to leave. Most of us wanted to go to America . . . that was our first goal.

"The Communists took everyone's money and made us exchange it for new currency with little value. Then they took over everything—small businesses, vendors' stalls, and factories." Indoctrination and "reform" programs were begun in the schools, including at the elementary level where Winston's father taught. "Things were pretty bad for our family," Winston recalled. "We were allowed to stay in the house we owned, but we had to pay rent to the government. Food and clothing were rationed, and the black markets spread . . . the cost of living kept going up . . . you couldn't do anything you wanted to. The state decided for you. We all realized we must get out."

The family finally agreed that Winston and his uncle, Nhan Luong, should make the first try, though everyone fully realized the risks they faced. Thousands of others had tried to make the trip by water; many had failed. Their departure was set for the night of August 22, 1978, a time that Winston will probably never forget. He was 15½ years old and about to begin his junior year in high school. But the time had come to break ties with the past, to leave his parents and brothers and head for a new life. After a tearful farewell, Winston bundled up a few clothes and joined his uncle for a short ride on their battered motorbike through the darkened streets of Saigon to the waterfront.

CHAPTER FIVE

It was raining hard, a relentless tropical rain that quickly soaked the pair to the skin as they rode to the pier, avoiding the few soldiers on patrol. They joined three dozen other refugees huddled in a shed to await boarding the ramshackle 32-foot fishing boat whose ancient motor was already idling unevenly. Finally, they all crowded into the foul-smelling cabin below deck for the illegal and dangerous voyage out into the stormy South China Sea and to freedom.

For Winston, this was the first leg of a 9,000-mile odyssey that would find him stranded for months in a transient camp in Malaysia and finally bring him to a prosperous farm community near Moline, Illinois, where he could begin his new life.

The voyage across 400 miles of open water to the Malay peninsula normally takes three or four days, but the refugees were at sea for nine days; all the food on board was ruined, and there was little water. Monsoonlike rains and heavy waves slowed and threatened to swamp the old boat.

Finally, on the morning of September 1 the engine failed altogether, and they wallowed helplessly in sight of the Malay coast for another day until the authorities towed them to safety in the lee of a small offshore island.

"It took us a few days to recover from that trip," Winston recalled. "I felt terrible—landsickness I guess it was. I couldn't walk right and nobody could eat anything."

He and his uncle settled into the primitive tent city that already housed thousands of refugees seeking asylum and hoping for transition to a new country. They did not know then that it would be a long, uncomfortable, and frustrating wait of nine months before they would leave. Like refugees the world around, in Africa, Palestine, or Lebanon, perhaps some on Ellis Island a century ago, they shared the common miseries of bad food, little water, rudimentary shelter, and no electricity. But together they nourished the powerful aspiration and dream of a better life in America or France or Australia—wherever their destiny might take them.

Winston's two great enemies at that point were boredom and "the system"—the red tape and confusion—that everyone fought. Families generally had a better chance of getting a sponsor, but as the lone member of his immediate family who had escaped, Lieu eventually managed to be classified an orphan pro tem, which speeded up the immigration procedure.

Meanwhile, however, he remained in the camp with few resources, no chance for schooling, and only an English-language dictionary to read.

"We spent lots of time swimming," he said, "but reading the dictionary gave us something constructive to do and we helped each other to build up some kind of vocabulary, at least. Plus, I had learned a little English from my cousin in Saigon before I left."

Winston remembered that during the long months in camp, he had often thought about happier days in Saigon and about his fundamental education there. "Until the Communists came everyone took an academic curriculum, and there was excellent teaching in math and science," he said. After they came, however, the curriculum was modified to include more vocational emphasis, and politically oriented teachers were brought in to advance communist philosophy and thinking. "Math and science," Winston noted, "they really couldn't change too much. In history and geography and other classes they could do more."

Communication with his family back in Saigon (now called Ho Chi Minh City) ranged from infrequent to nonexistent, though occasionally word got through that his parents and brothers were all right. As the months passed on the Malaysian island, Winston knew that his father continued to teach and his mother to work, and that Vi and Le remained in school. But none of them had any way of realizing that it would be nearly six years before the family could be reunited.

The self-reliance and persistence taught to Winston by his father, and his mother's parting words, "Be good and

CHAPTER FIVE

work hard for your goals," sustained the boy through difficult days in the camp and prepared him in many ways for the further loneliness and challenge that would come even after he reached the United States.

Once he got word in the early summer of 1979 that the U.S. Catholic Conference would sponsor his trip, Winston concentrated his thoughts and plans on what lay ahead. His vision of America had been shaped by fragmented and perplexing images, an incomplete and contradictory mosaic of great wealth, endless open spaces, towering cities, loud music, and large, loud people speaking a complex language in accents that ranged from ranch-style Texan to sidewalk-tough New Yorkese. He knew, though, that within this vast land there was opportunity for those who would take it, and room to grow.

He came face to face with reality on June 26, 1979, when his long flight ended in the Midwestern prairie city of Peoria, Illinois. A medium-sized farming and agricultural equipment center on the Illinois River, Peoria is about as typical of the United States as any single town could be. The question "How will it play in Peoria?" has always been a whimsical way of asking how it—a product, an idea, a play, or whatever—will please Middle America.

Winston had only a couple of summer months in the Peoria area to decompress and begin adjusting to the American scene before he moved about 95 miles west and north on I-74 to join his sponsoring family, William and Dana Honn, who lived in Moline, Illinois. There, on the banks of the Mississippi, he prepared to enter his first year of school.

The Honns, who were connected with a refugee agency, gave the young Vietnamese boy his first home in America, began to teach him more English, and helped him get a handle on a strange and new society.

His transition year of 1979–80 at the high school in Moline was one of anxiety and confusion. After several months he was shuttled to another host family in nearby Altona, and had to move to a different high school. He became intensely aware of his uniqueness, and of his separation by much more than distance from every aspect of the world that he had known so well before: from his close-knit family, his friends, and all the familiar sights, sounds, smells, and feelings of a tropical homeland. With the help of his sponsors and a special school course in English as a second language, Winston improved his vocabulary and skills. He excelled in the science and math courses, but he continued to be conscious of the different lifestyle of his classmates, and especially of their size and preoccupation with things physical—cars, tractors, sports. There were few other Asians in the area, but despite his sense of isolation, Winston concentrated on his studies, and slowly, perhaps imperceptibly, began his Americanization.

As he was finishing classes in Altona, Winston learned that his uncle Nhan and his family had been granted entrance to the United States and were coming to live in Norfolk, Virginia. He was determined to join them, and made plans to move to the Tidewater area in the summer.

The thriving and expanding metropolitan area of Norfolk seemed like more familiar territory to him, with its milder climate and streams and rivers flowing into the Chesapeake Bay. The large naval and military bases nearby also generated a continually changing and diverse population of families and students. Granby High School lies within a couple of miles of the Norfolk Naval Base and the headquarters for the U.S. Navy's Sixth Fleet and the NATO allies.

The two-story, red-brick school is set well back from the busy highway and separated from it by a buffer of lawn and shade trees, including magnolias. It is a product of the Federal Works Administration, completed in 1939, and looks pretty much like any other high school of that vintage, having a large Georgian facade at the main entrance, topped by a white cupola and bronze weathervane.

During its five decades Granby High has welcomed, as-

CHAPTER FIVE

similated, and educated several waves of students. It has survived integration, seems comfortable about its mixture of black and white students and teachers, and has begun to absorb new immigrants from Southeast Asia.

Inside the front entrance stand the usual trophy cases full of cups and plaques. The building opens onto two main wings with wide, well-lit hallways flanked by the inevitable banks of metal lockers. At critical junctions, teachers monitor the orderly flow of students, and carry out their time-honored hassling of those without proper passes. "We have things pretty well together here," said head counselor Walter Green. "It's a good school."

Winston Lieu may have arrived at Granby as a largely unknown quantity, but as counselors interviewed him and looked over his records of achievement the understanding between them grew.

"I took more English classes," Winston recalled, "and I became a lot more conscious of how the high school curriculum worked. Back in Moline I didn't even know how the grade-point system worked."

Walter Green remembered Winston's early days and his test scores, even with a language handicap. "He had an exceptional record, considering everything he went through," Green said. "He scored a notable 690 on the mathematics section of the SAT, and also received high marks on the Test of English as a Foreign Language, which he took at Granby. About the only flaws in his academic transcript are two D's recorded in Illinois, and these are understandable—one was in English 10, a subject he was still struggling to master, and the other in physical education, a subject to which he adjusted."

As usual, Winston demonstrated the kind of positive thinking that marks his character. "It was hard for me at first," he said, "taking PE . . . I knew I was different, my body was smaller, I was not used to running a mile or so every day, which we had to do." (He didn't comment on the effect of months in the refugee camp, the substandard food, the physical and mental stress of his travels, the separation from his family.) "But, I learned that it was more a matter of adjusting to the exercise. I was capable of doing it and eventually I think it was good for me. I have learned from this—it's another extension of doing your best, whether mental or physical."

In the wood-paneled reception room of Granby's guidance department hangs a plaque with a simple but cogent motto: Believe, Achieve, Succeed. The school now has about 1,500 students, 60 percent of whom are college-bound. To help in their planning and preparation for college and work, there are six full-time counselors. The guidance department also has an IBM computer system that is easily operated and accessible to students. One particularly useful feature is a Guidance Information System (GIS) program that enables students to survey a range of college requirements and options, course offerings, prerequisites, and so on. "The counselors were a big help to me at Granby," Winston said, "and working with the GIS on the computer really gave me an edge in deciding what majors I might want in college."

Entering Granby in the fall of 1980 as a 17-year-old junior, Winston soon adjusted to the academic demands of a full schedule, including chemistry, physics, English, history, and math. Within 10 days of his arrival in Norfolk, he got a job at a local fast-food chain, Feather 'N Fin, and began purposefully blocking out his time so he could work a daily 5 p.m.-to-midnight shift (sometimes longer on weekends) and begin to build up his bank account.

What kind of student was he? Did he have friends? "He made lots of friends," Walter Green recalled, "both American and Asian. He kept busy all the time. He didn't hang around a lot, he didn't have time." Other counselors remembered that he was well liked by both teachers and students, that he

CHAPTER FIVE

was highly motivated, quick, bright. "He was a hard worker, gifted in math," one said, "but you especially noticed his self-confidence, his determination to do everything well."

Before too many months had passed, Winston had saved enough to get one of the vital necessities of American life, a car. It was a beat-up Chevette, but nonetheless it enabled him to get around in the Norfolk area and to get to his job at the restaurant and to school. While he tended primarily to see fluorescent light in the labs, libraries, and lunchrooms, he did occasionally find time for some ultraviolet rays at nearby Virginia Beach.

In April 1981 Winston became assistant manager of Feather 'N Fin in charge of the night shift. He continued in that capacity for the next three years, on into his college days. "The work load increased," he said, "but working there was good for me in many ways. First, it paid pretty well. Second, it made me schedule my time. But maybe best of all, it brought me in touch with the real world, you know, people of all kinds."

Winston moved into his senior year with greater confidence in his steadily improving English and his demonstrated record of superior achievement in every other area of study. He continued to make his college and career plans with help from counselors, and he qualified for enrollment in a college-level class of Advanced Placement calculus, where his teacher was Mrs. Lynette Corley.

"It was only a small class of particularly able math students," she recalled, "but I would remember Winston anyway. He had great drive, great intensity, a real curiosity and a love of learning that you don't see in too many students.

"He was serious, but when you think about his background, what he had been through, you can understand that. He was an ideal student, really. The kind you always hope for."

Why don't more American students have this determination? What makes Winston run? What motivates him to excel? Mrs. Corley reflected on this.

"We have just as many excellent students. They have the ability. Lots of them do succeed." She paused, thinking perhaps of her own life, starting out as a student at Granby, getting her undergraduate degree and then a master's at the College of William and Mary. She's now head of the math department at Granby, in addition to her teaching duties.

"I think maybe some of our kids lack the spark, the special drive that pushes Winston. Maybe his personal experiences, the trauma, the fear, have underscored for him the value of education, how much it means. When he was finishing high school here he was living out his dream. He knew it could be done; he never doubted it."

"It's true," Winston said. "I've always had respect for learning, even before I started school. My father began teaching when he was only 19, and he loved it. Maybe it was contagious in a way. We wanted to learn everything we could. I remember when I was in the sixth grade, reading all about Thomas Edison and George Washington—we read a fair amount of Western literature even in elementary school." Winston pointed out that in Vietnam, at least in the days before the war, the elementary curriculum was extensive, and included language and literature, history and culture, as well as math and science.

Winston contemplated why America's ethnic Asians won the five top awards in the 1986 Westinghouse Science Talent Search although they represent only a small fraction (1.6 percent) of the U.S. population.

"I don't think it's basically genetic," he said. "Probably it relates more to cultural traditions, going back many centuries. Like I said, learning is important to us. We enjoy it."

After further thought, he added: "And I must say too that the closeness of the family unit—our dependence on one another—plays a big role."

CHAPTER FIVE

He paused, thinking perhaps of all those who were still in Vietnam. "Of course," he said, "there's one other thing motivating us, maybe the biggest of all. It's freedom, intellectual freedom, political—whatever. You have it here, and that's why we came."

The United Nations estimates that as many as 700,000 people fled Vietnam illegally between the time the war ended in 1975 until 1979 when the legal exodus program began under the supervision of the U.N. High Commissioner for Refugees. Now, although the perilous boat exodus continues, legal departures run over 25,000 a year, with most refugees headed for the United States, Canada, France, and West Germany.

As graduation from Granby High approached in June 1982, Winston saw his dream begin to take on some tangible proportions. He had finished ninth in a class of 335 seniors, and had won two prestigious scholarships that would enable him to attend college. When he looked back, Winston said that this time in his life, and the commencement exercises in particular, marked a critical turning point, one that stimulated him and gave him added motivation to excel.

"I was sitting there listening to the valedictorian speak and I said to myself, 'I could be up there giving that speech if I had worked a little harder.' I rationalized a bit, maybe, that my background and language problems had held me back. But I decided I could and would do better in college."

After looking over various options at places like MIT and the University of Virginia, Winston decided to remain in the Norfolk area where he could continue to live at home, and to enter the engineering program at Old Dominion University. "I talked to my advisers and thought it all over carefully. I decided ODU would be best for me. I wouldn't have to move again, and the scholarships made it appealing, too. ODU paid full tuition for four years, and their engineering school is excellent."

In addition to the ODU scholarship, he received another

award from the Tidewater Builders Association ($1,200 a year for four years) and he also won first place among all Norfolk high school students in a nationally sponsored mathematics competition. Though he was just over 18, Winston Lieu had reached a high plateau of achievement. But he had little time for contemplation, and certainly none for complacency. He was busy looking ahead, planning his college program, keeping up his job, and still remembering with great clarity the days in the Malaysian camp only three years before.

His family remained in Saigon, actively working toward their escape, and hoping to join him in the United States before his brothers were drafted for service in the army. Winston had sent them over $2,000 from his savings, along with some clothing and medicine, and he continued to work with the government and relief agencies to get his father, mother, and brothers into the pipeline.

The formative and demanding undergraduate years at Old Dominion went by quickly. Winston followed a regular curriculum with a major in electrical engineering. He took a number of courses in the humanities, and only English presented a problem for him. "I failed the writing exam twice," he remembered, "but that only made me more determined, so I took a special preparatory class that involved a lot of writing, and the next time around I passed the exam. That gave me a lot of confidence."

Some of Winston's friends from Granby moved on to ODU with him, and he expanded his ties and contacts in the Norfolk community. As assistant manager of the Feather 'N Fin outlet, he had additional responsibilities and long hours, but, Winston noted, "There's a big difference between high school and college class schedules. You have a lot more flexibility in college, more time of your own to arrange study, research, work, or whatever.

"It was a good period for me. I was extending my knowledge, beginning to look toward practical goals, and also con-

CHAPTER FIVE

tinuing to earn money that would help bring my family back together."

As he neared the end of his college career, Winston spent three months in the summer of 1985 working as an engineer assistant for the IBM Corporation in Endicott, New York. This experience gave him a preview of what his professional business career might be like and enabled him to get a feeling for a large corporation in action.

"It was a pleasant setting," he said, "maybe a little isolated—or insulated—I guess, but it was a real working environment. We were studying electromagnetic comparability, exploring the radiation problems emanating from computers and other equipment.

"But it wasn't all work. We had time to make some friends and relax. We lived in a student dorm and had access to a club where we could swim and play basketball. It was interesting, too, meeting students from other colleges and comparing notes."

Winston's graduation from Old Dominion University in mid-December 1985 was a doubly joyous occasion. He had completed his degree studies in only 3½ years, amassing 30 credits beyond the 120 normally required; he had put together a remarkable 3.98 grade-point average in a difficult major (electrical engineering) with a computer science minor; and he had, of course, finished first in his class of 600.

But much more important to him, when he looked out on the crowd of more than 5,000 gathered for the ceremonies in the field house, was the knowledge that seated together in one of the front rows were his father, mother, and two brothers, newly arrived in the country, a proud and resilient family, reunited after six years of difficult separation.

During his final months at ODU, Lieu had been sorting out job offers from various companies in different parts of the country. He evaluated them carefully, giving considerable weight to opportunities that would enable him to advance his education at the graduate level. In the end, he narrowed the choice to Texas Instruments, Inc., in Dallas, and AT&T Bell Laboratories in New Jersey. After visits to each, he chose Bell Labs.

His family decided to remain in the Norfolk area, where his father, Thuong, had begun a course in English as a second language under the auspices of the public schools. "As soon as he finishes that course," Winston reported, "he's aiming at the GED to certify his high school equivalency. I'm sure he'll make it. My brother Vi is in school, at Tidewater Community College. That will give him a good base for further study or work."

Early in 1986 Winston Lieu started working at the Bell Labs facilities, which are situated about 25 miles west of New York City on 300 acres of rolling green countryside not far from Morristown, New Jersey, and the Great Swamp. It is an area of expanding high-tech companies, and the Bell grounds include a number of security gates and some discreet but efficient-looking barbed-wire fences that surround buildings involved in government work.

He quickly settled into the challenging routine of his new work and soon started looking ahead again. This time his goal was graduate study at Southern Methodist University in Dallas, where the company was going to send him for a year to get his master's degree. Sitting on a comfortable sofa in the Bell Labs visitors' reception area, Winston Lieu discussed his plans. He wore blue jeans, running shoes, and a plain white sports shirt, with the mandatory ID badge dangling from a metal chain around his neck. He seemed pleased and enthusiastic about the job.

"We work a regular day," he said, "but sometimes we stay late or come in on Saturday if we need more time to check out a special thought or explore a new idea." His assignments included studying the advanced design aspects of portable and mobile cellular phones, seeking ways to give them greater range and, perhaps, to decrease their size.

He had been taking some graduate-level classes within

CHAPTER FIVE

the company structure to advance his own knowledge and help him gain an edge in the steadily increasing intellectual competition that he found among his peers.

"I'll be moving to Dallas in the fall to attend SMU and work toward my master's degree in electrical engineering," he said. "AT&T calls it their One Year on Campus program, and it's a great opportunity to move up. I'm sure it will be difficult, but I'm always interested in looking at new horizons, seeing other parts of the country, different people, meeting new teachers with fresh perspectives. Probably I'll return here at the end of the year—there's a deadline on completing the degree."

In May 1987 Winston returned to Bell Labs with his master's degree in hand. "It was a hectic 9 months," he reported, "what with moving back and forth from New Jersey to Texas, and the pressures of a new environment and an entirely different school. But getting the additional knowledge and the degree made it more than worthwhile. And, along with the work, living in the Dallas area was fun for me, as I expected.

"I still take my studies and my work very seriously. I've found that each time I reach a new level, there's always more to learn, and here at AT&T our challenges regularly focus on the relationship between theory and practical applications. We're always trying to move on to new frontiers. I guess that's a sample of what life is all about anyway, isn't it? Moving on to higher levels, meeting new challenges."

Did he ever think about returning to Vietnam? "No, not at all," he responded quickly. But, on reflection, he added, "Well, maybe in a few years as a tourist. It might be interesting to see what they have done. But I have no desire to go back. This is my country now. My future is here."

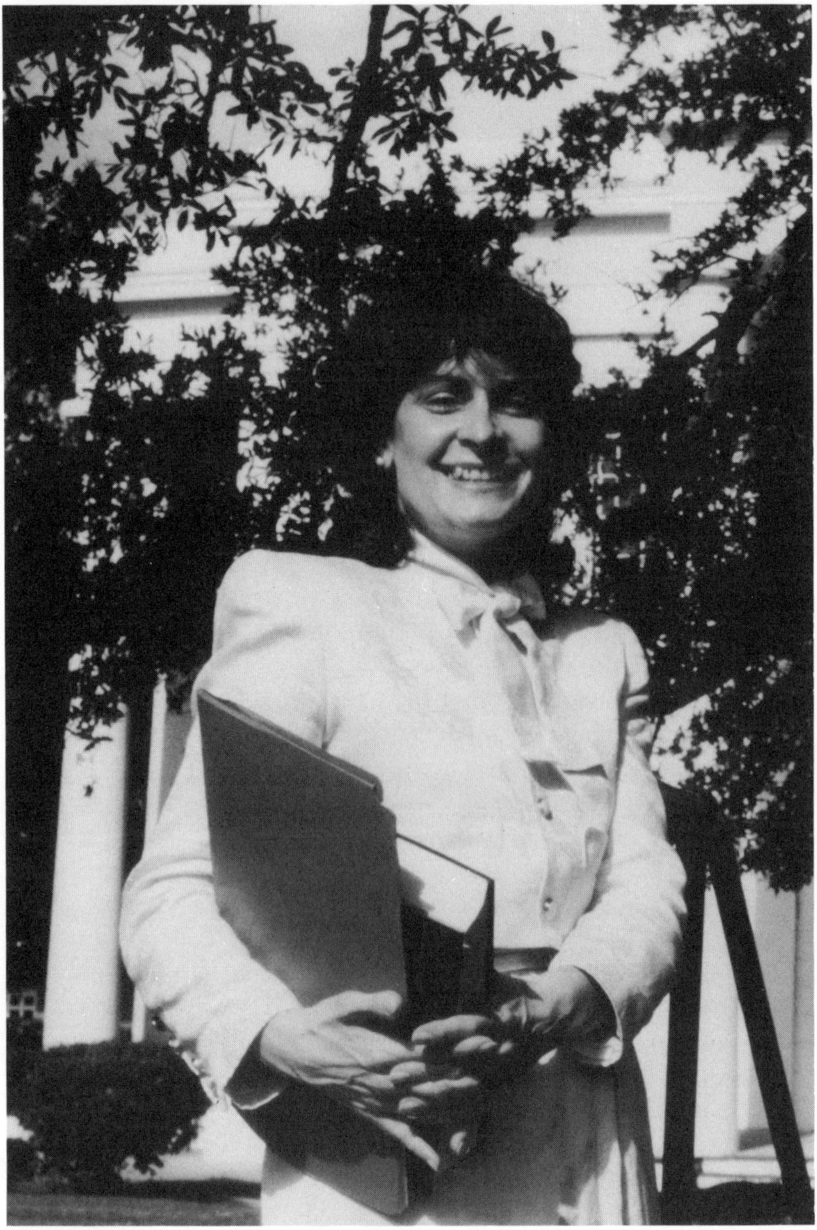

Chapter 6

SUZANNE SAUNDERS

Not much more than a dozen years ago, Suzanne Saunders was studying for her degree at the Mississippi School of Law in Jackson, working as a law clerk to gain experience, and waiting tables in Bernard's French restaurant to help support her family. During the Christmas season, partly as a joke, partly as a token of esteem, one of the local judges for whom she had worked presented her with a string tie, the clasp of which was a crested replica of that brash, energetic cartoon character, the Road Runner.

"I did run lots of errands around the courts," Suzanne remembered with a smile. "I was a real gofer. But I also ran titles and did legal research. That's the way I learned the ropes—some of the practical aspects of how law works, at ground level."

As she sat behind a large leather-topped desk in the comfortably furnished offices of her own legal firm on Old Canton Road in suburban Jackson, there was still a sense of restlessness about Suzanne Saunders, a feeling of controlled energy

CHAPTER SIX

looking for an outlet. "I've been that way since I was a child," she said. "My mother used to say I was driven. I was a free spirit, full of life and ambition—and some mischief."

That drive has taken her quickly to the top of a profession long dominated by men, and today she is one of about 100,000 female attorneys in the United States, a group that represents only 15 percent of all practicing lawyers.

The firm of Saunders, Abel, and Fortenberry enjoys wide respect in the capital city and around the state through its representation of such large businesses as the Wal-Mart Stores, Inc., and Liberty Mutual Insurance Company.

The road to success for Suzanne has been long and challenging, full of surprises, detours, and roadblocks, but she never wavered in her determination to finish her education, one difficult step at a time, or from a relentless pursuit of her career goals.

Despite her marriage at age 16 to David Cook and the birth of their first child between her junior and senior years of high school, she vowed to graduate with her class at Lafayette High School in Lexington, Kentucky, and did, shrugging off all stigmas, imagined or real, sometimes parking her infant son's buggy outside the classroom.

By the time she was 21, Suzanne had three children and was working her way through the University of Kentucky by holding down two full-time jobs. When her husband's job with IBM required a move to Jackson, Mississippi, she decided to attend law school there, and began working as a waitress to help meet expenses.

She had a superior record in law school and graduated cum laude. In the spring of 1976, she embarked on a remarkable legal career, specializing in insurance defense practice, and within two years had established her own firm. Since then, competing head to head in a tough but rewarding field, she has won a variety of honors and awards from both state and national groups, and has been admitted to practice before the U.S. Supreme Court, the Supreme Court of the State of Mississippi, and U.S. district courts in several jurisdictions.

Recently Suzanne Saunders took time out to reflect with pride and satisfaction—but not complacency—on her life thus far. Understandably, she has little patience for those who complain about how hard it is to finish school or find the money to pay for college. She has made her mark in a demanding profession. She's done it her way, the hard way, and she has paid her dues.

But little of the strife and uncertainty of the earlier years shows on her face. Seated in her tastefully decorated office, she wore a well-tailored mocha tan suit and a white broadcloth blouse, and talked confidently in a mid-Southern accent that still had traces of her early childhood days in Indiana and Michigan.

"I love the law," she said. "I relish court trials; the drama and excitement of having a case before a jury brings out my best. I realize every time I appear in court my reputation as a trial lawyer is on the line."

Framed on the walls were symbols of her success—degrees, credentials, awards, and tributes as well as handsome medieval brass rubbings. The room was also furnished with antique tables, twin porcelain lamps, deep pile carpets, and the inevitable rows of thick law books.

"I was always a difficult kid, I guess," she recalled. "I tended to resist authority, even my mom's. I wasn't intentionally bad, I was just asserting my independence."

Childhood memories of the Newton family remained fresh for one of her longtime friends, Gloria Baker Gadd of Lexington, who grew up in the same neighborhood, went through school with Suzanne, and has remained in close touch. "Suzanne's mother always put her down," Mrs. Gadd recalled. "They were on different wavelengths, I guess, and the antagonism seemed to have a strong role in shaping Suzanne's determination."

"I got paddled a lot," Suzanne said. "Both at home and

CHAPTER SIX

at school. I still remember the look of frustration on my first-grade teacher's face. I got lots of U's—for unsatisfactory—in conduct."

"There's no doubt Suzanne was strong-willed," Gloria Gadd commented. "Once she had made her mind up, she never wavered, and there was always a sense of logic in her arguments."

It took a while for Suzanne's energies to be channeled positively, but the sudden death of her father in a truck accident when she was 12 and her sister Rosalind was 9 had powerful emotional and financial effects on their lives. Suzanne remembered vividly the day they returned from the funeral home and Corinne Newton said to the sisters, "Well, girls, since your daddy's gone, we're not going to have very much, and whatever you want you'll have to earn for yourselves."

"What she meant was that we would be responsible financially," Suzanne said, "that we all had to carry our own weight. While she and I had lots of battles, she set an awfully good example for us when we were young. She was a college graduate, with a degree from Butler University in Indianapolis, but all the time we were in school she worked in a cafeteria washing dishes. It wasn't until later on that we realized she did this so she could be at home every day when we came back from school."

Suzanne lined up baby-sitting jobs during junior high school, and she also had a lawn-cutting arrangement with several neighbors. "That girl was always working," Gloria remembered. "She seemed to have an excess of energy and vigor, and it was a good thing, because she mowed lawns all over the area, and I'm not talking little lawns, either."

As she moved toward high school, Suzanne was an average student, nothing outstanding. "She was a pretty good student, I would say," Gloria recalled. "But she wasn't a grind, she didn't spend all her time in the library. Having friends and being popular were more important things to her in those days."

During the early 1960s, the Newton family lived in Lexington, Kentucky, the prosperous hub of the state's thoroughbred-horse empire, a city set in a countryside of gently rolling hills and neatly laid-out farms, with whitewashed rail fences, barns and stables with distinctive triple cupolas, and names and architecture recalling the French settlers of the area.

On the lush pasture land outside town roam stallions and mares from Calumet Farms, Bold Meadows, and a score of legendary places where champions are bred and born. Nearby villages like Versailles and Paris preserve the French connection and so does Lafayette High School, which Suzanne attended.

Lafayette is a large two-story red-brick structure with neat white trim on the windows, situated on a slight rise in the midst of well-kept homes and park land. The school colors are red, white, and blue, and the yearbook is named *The Marquis;* the athletic teams compete under the name the Generals. Needless to say, the French Club thrives.

"Once I got into high school, I plunged into a lot of activities," Suzanne said. "I didn't really study too much in the early years, but I never had any real problems. My best subjects were math and science, but I seemed to reach a plateau in math, and that eventually kept me from majoring in chemistry, which I liked. I was on the swim team, and I was into cheerleading. But I really concentrated on having a good time. I chased boys."

The 1965 edition of *The Marquis* shows Suzanne as a smiling, attractive girl with softly curled hair swept back from her face. In addition to swimming, she was in the choir, the French Club, and the Future Homemakers of America.

During 1965 the band won the state championship, the senior play *(Pillow Talk)* made $453 for the class, and the

CHAPTER SIX

basketball coach, newly hired, was Adolph F. Rupp, Jr., son of the famed University of Kentucky coach.

Lafayette was and remains probably about as typically American as a high school can be, a good place to prepare for life and careers. Sixty-seven percent of the graduating seniors in 1965 went on to college, and Suzanne was among them. But there were some complications.

One began, perhaps, at the skating rink. "It was a popular place for kids much of the year," Gloria Gadd remembered. "They would gather there in summer to be at the pool and hang around, play games. In winter, there was skating if it got cold enough. That's where Suzanne and David Cook met."

"I loved ice skating," Suzanne said, "but we didn't have much money, so I took a job at the rink to make a little cash and I got to skate free. That's where I met David. He was a *much* older man, all of 20, but he had finished school and was working for IBM. My mother and I finally agreed on something: he was wonderful. We dated for a year or so before getting married. Mom had let me date early, not much over 12, I guess, but she had no choice. I probably would have gone out anyway. That's the way I was, headstrong."

David Cook had gone to work for IBM after he finished high school and the company was helping him pay for the courses he was taking at the University of Kentucky. Though Suzanne was only 16, marriage seemed a logical and certain course to both of them. They were married in Lexington in 1963. Halfway through her junior year, Suzanne dropped out of school, and later, while she was taking summer school classes, her first son was born. True to her determination, she reentered Lafayette in September to finish her senior year on schedule.

"Suzanne and David had some hard times when they were first married," Gloria recalled. "They lived with the Cooks for a while. They didn't have much money at all, but they got a small apartment just before the baby was born. Suzanne's attitude was incredible, so positive, so determined. She said to herself—and to the world: 'Yes, we have this baby, and now we're a family, and we're going to get on with it, get back to school.' When September came, she was ready to go back and she did."

While she was at home with the baby, Suzanne started taking correspondence courses from the University of Kentucky to fill in her high school requirements and as the fall term approached, she went to Lafayette and talked with her counselor, Warren Featherston, who later went on to become a high school principal in Lexington. She felt sure Lafayette would welcome her return to classes, and it did, but Mr. Featherston had some words of caution. Suzanne still remembered this encounter.

"When I told him I wanted to come back and graduate with my class, he said, 'That's fine, Suzanne, but you must understand that you're not to talk to the other students about things married people talk about.' Once I recovered, I said, sure, no problem. And it worked out. But society today is a lot more liberal than it was then, some 20 years ago. You just weren't supposed to talk then about anything that remotely hinted at sex in a marriage."

She recalled the first days back. "It wasn't easy, the baby was only a few months old. I took him to school sometimes, and left his buggy outside the classroom. A bit later on, after David and I adjusted our school and work schedules, I had a sitter for him. Believe it or not, I made good grades in my senior year, very good grades. And it was interesting to see the reactions around school. I think I was more accepted by the kids after the baby than I had been before."

Gloria Gadd said, "Credit that to her positive attitude. It affected everyone else's attitude, and everyone—students and teachers—developed real respect for what she was doing."

"I can still remember hearing the senior girls talk about where they were going to college," Suzanne noted, "about what their majors would be, and what sorority rushes they might consider. I knew right then that they weren't going on

CHAPTER SIX

without me. I wanted to be a college graduate, and my mother agreed. She had always encouraged us and expected us to finish school. My sister graduated from Western Kentucky University and went into teaching."

Suzanne Saunders paused in her reflections on those earlier days as a high school senior and looked around her comfortable modern office with its neatly arranged magazines and reference books. "You know, as I approached graduation and my son had his first birthday, I started thinking seriously—for the first time maybe—about the future, about where my life was heading. I said, 'Suzanne, when this boy is 20 and gone from home, you will be 37 years old. What are you going to do with your life?' I knew then that I would never be satisfied as a housewife; I knew I had to have something to fall back on, a career, more challenges.

"I thought my best hope was somehow to make a transition to the University of Kentucky, which was right in Lexington, only a mile or two away. I had begun to take correspondence courses, but one necessary subject terrified me—freshman composition, which everyone had to pass. I was a slow reader, a poor speller, and not a very good writer. I was scared to death of failing; I had heard all the stories of how they weed out freshmen in these composition classes. So I decided to take the course on campus and face it head on. This meant a lot of sacrifices."

Thus began several difficult and demanding years for Suzanne and her family. At age 18 she started at the university on a part-time basis. While her husband continued to work, she organized a baby-sitting service for the academic year, from September to June, and looked after six children, including her own, in their one-bedroom apartment.

"It was pretty hectic," Suzanne recalled. "Playpens everywhere. It was a nursery of sorts and I charged something like $10 or $15 per child per week, so that wasn't bad income, maybe $90 a week."

She survived, and the next year, she and David took the

money earned from the nursery enterprise and bought their first house in Lexington. By the time Suzanne was 19, her second child, Emily, had been born and it had also become clear that she was running out of evening and correspondence courses at the university. "I had to figure out a way to attend full time, during the days, and that did take some juggling, because we needed more money for my tuition and books, and to pay for our son David, who was in the Montessori school by then. That's when I started working at two full-time jobs and still attending classes. When I look back on it now, I'm not sure how I did it."

Her schedule seemed to use up more hours than there were in a day. She would feed the kids an early dinner and go to work as a waitress at The Springs, a local restaurant and inn favored by the crowd of horse breeders, traders, and others involved in Lexington's favorite sport. It's a pleasant and comfortable Colonial-style place on Harrodsburg Road, not far from the university, and convenient to many farms and the major racing arena and stables of Keeneland.

"The Springs became her home away from home," Gloria recalled. "She enjoyed the atmosphere and the people on the staff. The tips were wonderful, especially during the horse meetings every spring and fall. And she also got her meals there and sometimes the cook gave her bones for her dog."

One of the longtime waitresses at the restaurant remembered Suzanne well. "She was always friendly and full of energy. She still comes by here whenever she visits Lexington. You know, in those days her family didn't have much money. She told me she bathed all the kids at one time to save water."

After working a full dinner shift from 4:30 p.m. until 10 or 10:30 p.m., Suzanne would drive across town to her second job as a checker at the Shopper's Choice grocery. "I worked there until dawn," she said, "and fortunately there were slow periods when I could study a little and get some reading done. I got home in the morning in time to help David get the kids up and dressed, and then the cycle started over.

CHAPTER SIX

"When did I sleep? On alternate days, whenever I could catch a nap. I slept on Tuesdays, Thursdays, and Sundays, the way my schedule worked out. It's all a matter of organization; I like to call it dovetailing. Make the best use of your time and energy. When the kids were older, I tried to give them some lessons on how to coordinate things, get priorities straight, take full advantage of their resources. It can be done. I'm living proof."

There was not a lot of time left over for other things. "We didn't have many luxuries or extras. I guess I saw only two movies the whole time I was going through college—*The Graduate* and *Romeo and Juliet*. Now when I look back on those days I get to laughing. We had tough times, but we had fun, too. We were on a tight budget. I had to create some ingenious meals."

"Suzanne could get more miles out of one chicken than anyone I ever knew," Gloria recalled. "I remember those meals. First, they would have roast chicken, then chicken salad, then chicken hash ... and later, from the bones, chicken noodle soup. She was a frugal planner, but skillful; she counted her pennies."

"We never went hungry," Suzanne said. "We also ate lots of frozen potpies. They were cheap then, maybe 20 for a dollar; they were easy and fast and not a bad diet either—plenty of meat and vegetables. They filled you up, too. But now I never eat them!"

It took Suzanne the better part of six years to complete her undergraduate degree with a major in textiles, clothing, and merchandising from the College of Home Economics at the university. Despite her earlier struggles in math, she minored in chemistry.

One of her instructors at the time, Dr. Charlotte Bennett, now a dean at North Dakota State University in Fargo, vividly recalled Suzanne—her strong personality, her academic interests, and, above all, her determination. "Electric is the word that comes to mind when I think of having Suzanne in class. An extremely high energy level marked everything she did, in and out of class. I watched her winning a struggle 'against all odds,' with her small children, a husband, and limited financial resources. I came to admire her dedication and brightness, and her joy in experiencing life.

"She never asked for special privileges because of family responsibilities or work obligations. Many women in her circumstances would not have ventured out of the home to build a professional future back in the late 1960s. She turned her back on convention . . . and plowed through college degree requirements in true style.

"I remember in those days her unique ability to master the fundamentals of merchandising and then apply these to her own life through some limited but successful ventures in real estate. From some of her earnings as a waitress, she bought a small piece of land on the outskirts of Lexington, subdivided it, and sold it shortly thereafter for a profit."

Upon finishing her undergraduate degree, Suzanne began a few graduate courses, including research into man-made fibers. "But I got bored and focused more on merchandising," Suzanne recalled. "Then when I realized that some of my most important decisions on a job in that field would involve such things as helping decide what color undergarments women would be wearing next year, I realized that a change of direction was needed—this was not what I had in mind for my future."

Some of her friends in Lexington, including attorney Tom Bunch, whom she had met when her son attended the Montessori school, urged her to consider another transition, this time from merchandising to the law.

"My studies in retail merchandising, like most things you learn in school, were not wasted," Suzanne observed. "This knowledge has come in very handy during my law practice here because our firm represents a number of large compa-

CHAPTER SIX

nies and department stores in Jackson and around the state. I think my university work gave me a better understanding of their methods and needs."

As Suzanne contemplated possible options during 1972, her husband's company (IBM) transferred him from the Lexington area to Jackson, and they prepared to move. By that time they had three young children (Joseph had been born during the college years), and increasingly their goals and career plans seemed to be diverging. "I guess we were simply too different," Suzanne said. "David really had no interest in any further education. I felt it was essential for future income and career plans. His lack of motivation frustrated me. We had lots of good times together, and some bad. David's a solid individual, a good father and husband. We were simply on different tracks. We stayed together for the move, and for some time after that, but we knew it would not last."

For Suzanne and the family, a new series of challenges began with their move to Jackson, a modern city of nearly a quarter million, with a proud history as a pillar of the Old South, founded by the French-Canadian trader Louis LeFleur on the west bank of the Pearl River, and named state capital in 1821.

Once established in Jackson, Suzanne focused her attention on further education and decided to enter the Jackson School of Law (now known as Mississippi College School of Law). This involved once again shaping complex schedules that took her through a succession of long days filled with classes, study, and family responsibilities—David, Emily, and Joseph were moving through school—and nights waiting tables at Bernard's, a popular French restaurant in town.

Suzanne again had to call on her deep reserves of energy. Her fascination with the law grew, and she took an unpaid summer position with the firm of Daniel, Coker, Horton & Bell as a clerk and general factotum. "I did everything," she remembered, "detail work, legal research, pleadings. The experience was priceless. About halfway through law school,

I actually began to try some cases, with the permission of the court. It was sort of an advanced internship; someone else's name appeared on the records, but I did the courtroom work, and I took to it immediately. I loved the challenge."

She also became involved in a steadily expanding number of activities related to her legal education, including becoming treasurer of the Student Bar Association, the student division of the American Bar Association, and the alumni editor of *Amicus Curiae*, a Jackson School of Law publication.

Suzanne continued working at an intensive pace and completed her law degree, with honors, in a little over three years. But during 1976-77, in the thirteenth year of her marriage, she faced what she has called two of the three main traumas of life at once: divorce and the loss of a job. The cumulative strains and tensions of Suzanne's and David's diverging lifestyles and goals had finally reached a point of no return. They agreed to separate amicably; the children remained with her. Their divorce settlement contained a unique clause that perhaps characterizes as well as anything the nature of their mercurial times together. "The terms require that we dance together once a year in each 10-year period," Suzanne said. "I know it sounds strange and romantic, but we used to dance a lot together; we danced competitively, in contests. The judge who granted the divorce found it a little hard to believe, and we haven't actually carried out the dancing. But the principle was important to me—to us."

Upon graduation, she had taken a full-time job with Daniel, Coker, Horton & Bell and had begun to get involved in the complex and highly competitive litigation work of insurance defense. She thrived on it, and she also started to broaden her bar activities, working with state groups providing legal aid to disaster victims, and, later, with workmen's compensation issues.

In this period, Suzanne grew closer to her teenage children. She continued to insist on rigorous but reasonable rules and guidelines that were mutually acceptable. "One of the

CHAPTER SIX

kids once characterized me as a combination of mother and master sergeant," Suzanne reported, and that's probably not too inaccurate; organization and discipline had become essential in her tightly structured life.

"I worried that they might watch too much TV when I was working," she remembered. "Sometimes I took the TV set and locked it in the trunk of my car just to be sure."

She reflected on her own relationship with her mother, her early dating, her headstrong behavior. "I guess it's understandable, and maybe ironic, that I have always been pretty strict with my kids as they grew up. I wouldn't let them date young, for whatever reason. My oldest son, David, for instance, never had—or wanted, I guess—a date until his senior prom in high school. He didn't have a car, which no doubt played a part in that . . . he rode his bike around until he was about 20. But I don't believe in simply giving kids cars; they must earn them on their own.

"Emily had her first date—for the junior prom—when she was about 16. And Joe, who's a high school senior, has had a few dates, mainly this year. So I guess it's working out all right.

"David has finished undergraduate studies at Millsaps College in Jackson and now plans to do graduate work in computer science, maybe in Texas. Emily's a sophomore at Delta State in Mississippi. She's an art major and doing well. Joe, of course, is just finishing up high school, so we're not sure where he will head." Not one of them has yet expressed an interest in legal studies, though all have been supportive of their mother's work and proud of her progress.

Gloria Gadd, who remains in touch with Suzanne on a regular basis, offered further commentary on the family relationships. "Once when she and Emily were having a problem, Suzanne told me how stubborn the girl could be, and I reminded her that she might, in fact, be her mother's daughter. That struck home. But while she's always been strict with the kids, she's always been fair. She never expected from them anything that she herself would not give, and she would give *more.*

"When she and her son David talked about higher education, or additional studies, she told him 'I'll help you pay for Harvard, but not the University of Mississippi.' I guess this reflects her value judgments and her preoccupation with excellence."

During 1977 Suzanne faced the second of her traumas. In the course of her professional work, she had met and become friends with Hubbard T. Saunders IV, a prominent local attorney whose firm had ties with U.S. Senator James Eastland. As their friendship developed while her divorce proceedings were still underway, Daniel, Coker, Horton & Bell decided that the delicate social and business interrelationships obliged them to let her go.

"Probably it was for the best," Suzanne said. She believes the firing gave her just the motivation she needed to branch out, diversify, and, eventually, to start her own business. "It was a real stroke of fortune that helped put me in control of my own life," she realized later. "Of course, I may not have seen it entirely that way at the time."

She and Hubbard Saunders were married later in 1977, and when she was ready to begin private practice, he stood ready to assist. "He has been my silent senior partner," Suzanne said. "He gave me and my new firm important moral support at a critical time."

She continued to broaden her experience with various law groups in Jackson, learning (among other things) the intricacies of oil and gas abstracting. By the spring of 1978, Suzanne was ready to open her own office and concentrate on insurance defense.

An interesting alliance of men helped sustain her during the difficult early days. Elmo Speckles and James Smith, two oil-company officials she met while doing research on oil and gas contracts, helped supply her with enough work to keep her fledgling offices open. Then David Hart of Liberty Mutual

CHAPTER SIX

Insurance Company and John Carbone from Travelers Insurance came along to be among her first clients. "They had the guts and courage to trust me with their work when there was no basis for believing that I would succeed."

It soon became clear, however, that Suzanne Saunders had exactly the right combination of educational background, practical experience, and temperament to enable her to move with confidence and success into the courtroom arena. Now she can point with pride to a string of victories; she has lost only one case in all the time she has been defending insurance companies.

"Success means having the jury come in with the right verdict for our case," she said. "But it takes a lot of care and preparation every time. I feel very strongly about covering every conceivable base before a trial. I do my homework in great detail, and then I do a little bit more. I'm always fine-tuning the skills I have. I'm a kind of no-nonsense, nose-to-the-grindstone lawyer, but that's what pays off in the end. I enjoy having those 12 people in a box where they can't get away."

During the late 1970s and early 1980s, as her practice expanded and her reputation as a successful trial attorney became known throughout the state, Suzanne was increasingly involved in professional activities of the American Bar Association and state legal groups. She served on several committees of the ABA and was named in 1980 to be a member of the Special Commission on Advertising of the ABA. In recent years she has been a guest lecturer on legal ethics at the Mississippi College of Law and has taught advanced trial techniques at a national legal institute in Washington, D.C.

Suzanne was listed among the Outstanding Young Women of America in the years 1979–82, and in 1984 *Esquire* magazine selected her as one of the "best of the new generation—men and women under 40 who are changing America," along with others like actress Meryl Streep, playwright Beth Henley, and Dr. J (Julius Irving).

SUZANNE SAUNDERS

In December 1986 the widely read ABA *Journal* carried a cover story about the role of women in law today, and the banner line quoted from a Chicago circuit judge read: "I don't think that ladies should be lawyers." The article reported on the trials and tribulations of women lawyers around the country, including Suzanne Saunders. Most of those quoted felt that gender bias was not a burning issue, but a few had experienced outright prejudice. Suzanne said she feels that "being a woman has worked in my favor." She noted that whether in courtrooms or chambers, judges and attorneys alike have treated her equitably, and added that in Mississippi she is often referred to as "Miss Suzanne," which she takes as a form of endearment and respect. "It's a way of speaking, a regional pattern that shows the jury how highly the judge thinks of me. I try cases in 'the boonies,' sparsely settled rural areas of the state, and people just don't treat ladies ugly in places like that."

When rare problems suggesting sexism do arise, she recommends that lawyers shrug it off, "not be too thin-skinned, not take themselves too seriously." She and her female cohorts, now representing some 40 percent of all law school graduates, have, indeed, come a long way from the days in the 1870s when a U.S. Supreme Court opinion by Justice Joseph P. Bradley denied aspiring lawyer Myra Bardwell of Illinois the right to practice law, asserting that "the paramount destiny and mission of women [is] to fulfill the noble and benign offices of wife and mother."

What's next for Suzanne Saunders? In 1984 she told interviewers she was content with her present situation. "As a young person, I had many, many goals and most of them have been attained." Not long ago she told Gloria Gadd that maybe she had been working too hard, that maybe it was time to step back and reassess her life, and spend more time with her husband and family. But, on the other hand, she has also characterized herself as "a lawyer's lawyer, always honing what skills I have. I want the big cases now, I'm no

CHAPTER SIX

longer content with the fender-benders."

There has been a satisfying sense of unity to her life. She's come full cycle from the problems and crises of her childhood, school days, and first marriage, to enjoy a thriving law practice and to see her own children finish school and college and move on to careers. The discipline and determination of the earlier days have, indeed, paid off.

And still the inner voice is talking to her. She's always looking for the next challenge. "I've given some thought to branching out, maybe into business," she said recently. "I have my eyes open for opportunities in corporations, for instance. I wouldn't mind being chief executive of the right company. . . . I think I could do a good job in certain fields, with my diverse background. I've explored a few possibilities."

Though she is far from dissatisfied with the modern offices of Saunders, Abel, and Fortenberry at One Le Fleur's Square, with their atrium garden, flowing fountain, and handsome redwood walls, Suzanne Saunders is always thinking ahead. For some time she had had her eye on the imposing white-columned Greek revival mansion of former governor Ross Barnett. Late in 1986 she negotiated its purchase, and after some renovation, she and her associates plan to move in during 1988. "I think the place will make appropriate and comfortable quarters for our group," she said. "Somehow, the idea of Govenor Barnett's mansion just appeals to me."

Whether the appeal is symbolic or practical remains to be seen. But those will not be bad quarters for a former skating rink attendant, waitress, aspiring law clerk, and first-class road runner.

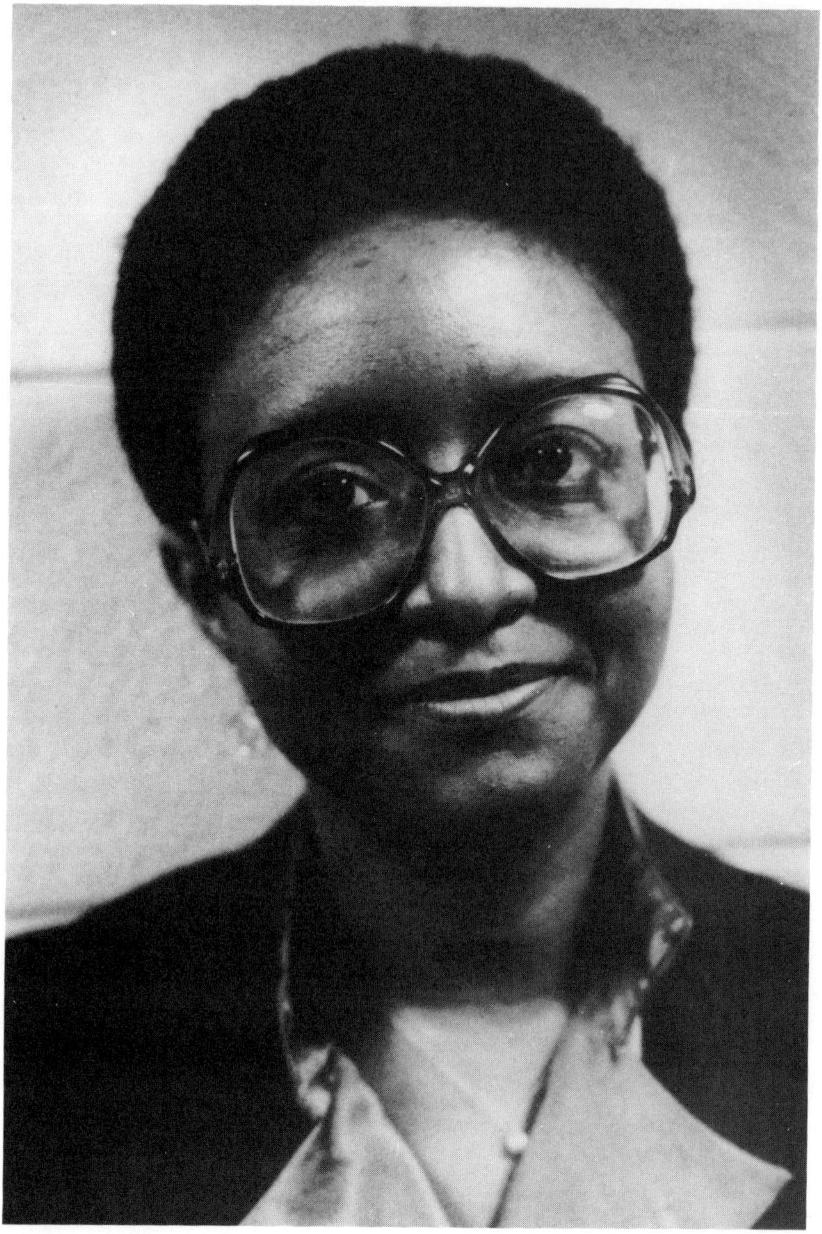

Chapter 1

SYBIL JORDAN STEVENSON

It looked and seemed pretty much like any one of the thousands of high school graduations taking place around the country in late May 1962. On a warm spring evening, ceremonies were under way in the lighted football stadium behind Central High School in Little Rock, Arkansas.

As the crowd of students, parents, and friends filed into the seats, they had every reason to be proud of the 523 graduates; almost all of them were college-bound and they had won more than their share of honors and awards.

One by one the seniors paraded across the athletic field to receive their diplomas. Then, as 17-year-old Sybil Jordan reached the podium, her dark gown neatly pressed, her tasseled cap squarely in place, a murmur rippled through the audience, followed by a derisive whistle or two and nervous laughter.

The young woman quietly took her diploma, shook hands with principal Jesse Matthews, and returned to her seat, impassive, but stung by the stage whispers from her class-

CHAPTER SEVEN

mates: "Here comes the nigger now. . . . She finally made it. . . . I guess Black Beauty's happy now."

Sybil Jordan ranked near the top of her class, 1 of 52 honor graduates that night, was the only black among them, the first and only black to complete an entire high school career at Central, and the winner of a four-year scholarship to Earlham College. Her victory had not been an easy one. It had come after three years of isolation and indignity, of apprehension and fear, of determination and courage.

The ordeal at Central High had actually begun some five years earlier when Governor Orval E. Faubus had defied a federal court order to start integration of the school, and ordered the Arkansas National Guard to blockade Central and prevent nine black students from entering. Faubus precipitated what some have called "the most serious constitutional crisis since the Civil War," and subsequent events caused President Dwight D. Eisenhower to federalize the National Guard and send regular army troops (the 101st Airborne Division) to Little Rock to bring stability and order to the town.

After a tumultuous and disruptive year of intermittent successes and setbacks during 1957–58 that severely strained relationships between the city's black and white communities, the Arkansas legislature closed all of the city's four high schools in a show of "massive resistance," and not until the fall of 1959 did Central High open again.

For a quarter of a century, the comprehensive high school had been the pride of the capital city, a modern, well-designed building with an excellent faculty and a college-bound rate of over 90 percent. Until 1957 it was for whites only. Most black students attended Horace Mann across town, also a good school that traditionally prepared many of its students for careers and professions.

Entering in 1959 as a tenth grader, Sybil Jordan began her long, lonely path in an alien atmosphere, surrounded by some 1,800 white students and always under the watchful eye of soldiers.

She remembers the early days when she first approached the imposing five-level structure of sand-colored brick and stone and climbed the ornate stairways leading to the main entrance. As she neared the doors, she glanced up at four mystical figures carved in stone above the Italianate archway, and still clearly recalls the four words inscribed there: ambition, personality, opportunity, preparation.

Those words carried more direct and personal meaning for Sybil than for almost any other student in the school. She entered full of ambition and personality. "It was her own decision to go," her mother said. "She knew she could make it." Through her bittersweet experiences at Central, Sybil Jordan sought to gain both preparation and opportunity; she made school history, Arkansas history, and became one of the real pioneers in the nation's emerging civil rights movement of the early 1960s.

From the crucible of Central High School she extracted the skills, the understanding, and the toughness that carried her to college and beyond to graduate degrees, a teaching and administrative career in higher education, and the position of corporate executive.

Today when you read Sybil Jordan Stevenson's official biography from GTE or scan entries about her in the various *Who's Who*s, there is little mention of her high school experiences in Little Rock. But those traumatic years left an indelible stamp on her life, helped shape her character, and influenced both her educational and professional careers.

Not only did she survive at Central High, she prospered, grew, and was enriched by the experiences. While the scars remain, some deep, some invisible, she has overcome her trials through a nobility of spirit that continues to grace her life today.

From her tenth-floor office in the gleaming glass-and-

CHAPTER SEVEN

stone compound of GTE in Stamford, Connecticut, Sybil looked out over the sparkling waters of Long Island Sound, dotted with a handful of white sails, and talked about her early life.

"I guess a combination of things got me where I am today," she said. "A strong, supportive family, involvement in community and church activities, some excellent and dedicated teachers, and my own stubbornness, my desire to be the best.

"There was never a question of *what* I was going to do after high school, just a matter of *where* I was going to do it. Sometimes life was lonely, but my parents were always nearby with an upbeat message when I needed it. They were strong-willed and they lived strictly according to their principles."

As manager of the corporate contributions program at GTE, a giant telecommunications group, Sybil Stevenson supervises the distribution of some $9 million yearly to colleges and universities around the country. She carries out a hectic schedule of travel and writing and speaking commitments.

In Stevenson's modern, functional quarters there is a big plan-a-date calendar on one wall. A small bookshelf is full of GTE publications, manuals, and education directories. On the far wall is a map of the United States highlighting GTE offices and operations, and an unobtrusive computer terminal stands in one corner. One of the few decorations on her neat desk is a small lucite owl, an ancient symbol of wisdom.

Sybil is about 5'3", slender, animated, self-possessed, and witty. Her conversation is sprinkled with educational terms, business jargon, and occasional colloquialisms derived from the years of working with urban students in Chicago and New York. Only a faint undertone of her Arkansas accent remains, muted by the years of living elsewhere and the discipline of many public-speaking engagements.

"I know I've come a long way, but sometimes I wonder if society has kept up. There are lots of disturbing things in the papers these days about a resurgence in racism, and not just in the South," Sybil noted with a tone of sadness and irony. She was referring to the stories about isolated but fairly widespread incidents on college campuses—Klan attacks at The Citadel in South Carolina; racist graffiti in the classroom of a black professor at the University of Colorado; hostility and tension at Yale; scuffles on the Amherst campus of the University of Massachusetts and at Ohio State University. One black student at the University of Texas in Austin recently said he felt that blacks there were *"on* the campus and at the university, but not *of* it."

"We have made a lot of progress since Central High," Sybil said, "but there are signs the momentum is fading a little; there's a loss of dedication, or conviction, maybe. The support and enthusiasm don't seem the same."

Sybil's parents, Leslie and Lorraine Jordan, both graduated from Philander Smith College in Little Rock, only a few blocks away from where they now live. Her mother later returned to the University of Arkansas and earned a master's degree in education. The family's educational roots go back further, too. Sybil's grandfather attended Alcorn A & M for three years at the turn of the century, but never completed his degree. Leslie Jordan works for the U.S. Postal Service, a job he took after leaving the army in 1945.

"Those were traditional things to do in Arkansas, in the South, in those days," Sybil said. "Either you were a teacher or you worked for the post office. Ironically, during all the days of strife at Central High, including the time Sybil attended, her father's route regularly took him into the school for deliveries, sometimes under armed escort. ("Neither rain nor snow nor heat. . . .")

Sybil achieved the first of her many firsts by being the first black baby born in the Springfield, Missouri, hospital. Her father was stationed at nearby Fort Leonard Wood when she was born. After her father was sent on overseas duty to Okinawa, Sybil returned from Springfield with her mother

CHAPTER SEVEN

to settle in Little Rock. They lived in the Capitol Hill area, a neighborhood of modest single-family homes between Seventh and Eighth streets, not far from the splendid Batesville granite-and-marble capitol building, which is modeled after the U.S. Capitol. Now, freeways have replaced many of the landmarks they knew so well.

"I grew up in a wonderful neighborhood," Sybil recalled. "My family owned a small grocery in a mixed residential area, and there were good feelings of community then. There was a white grocery on a nearby corner; some of the block was white, some black. Salesmen came and went; there was a mix of customers. We felt compatible; there was separation, but there was interaction.

"I worked in the store from the time I was tall enough to get up on a stool. I learned to operate adding machines and the cash register. I kept the books. And when I was about six or seven, I got my own paper route."

"She delivered Daisy Bates's paper, the *Arkansas State Press,*" her mother said. "She and her brother, Leslie, Jr., both had routes, and they managed their own money."

"It was great experience," Sybil added. "I learned early to talk to people, meet them on equal terms."

But there were other realities. "We had many friendly relationships," Sybil continued. "There was a sense of dignity, but a sense of place, too. You knew you wouldn't be invited to dinner, for instance. And when I went downtown on the bus to pay bills, I knew I would sit in the back."

Lorraine Jordan recalled those times with a touch of sadness. "The kids knew the limits and the boundaries, both physical and social. They knew they couldn't go downtown for a soda, for example."

"Little Rock was that kind of town then," Sybil said, "but I loved it. I don't think I could be the person I am today except for all the collective experiences, the collective strengths of that community. I am who I am today not only because of my parents, but also because of the kind of place I lived in.

"All these disparate parts come together to make it possible for me to live in this larger world today." She gestured around the modern office complex and the splendid view over Long Island Sound, as she reflected on her personal achievements.

The Jordan home was a supportive environment for Sybil and her brother, who was just 18 months younger than she and who followed her through grade school and into Central High.

"We always had plenty of books around as the children were growing up," Lorraine Jordan recalled. "There were bookcases up and down the stairs, everywhere. Sybil always loved books, and they both read a lot. We had one of the early TV sets, and we went to the movies when we could."

"I remember the first television shows," Sybil said. "But you know what sticks in my mind more was the whole family sitting around listening to radio. We listened to Jack Benny and Amos and Andy . . . and my own favorite was the Shadow. When TV came, we watched Ed Sullivan and Bob Hope.

"I went to elementary school and Dunbar Junior High right in my neighborhood. We could walk there, and that's one reason I wanted to go on to Central. It was nearby, in my part of town, and it was excellent. Horace Mann, the black high school, was good, too, but it was way on the other side of town. Most of my friends went there, of course, and being alone became one of my biggest challenges at Central. I couldn't be in any clubs, couldn't attend the games or be in the band.

"We had really good teachers in the early grades. I came to appreciate this more later on, because I realized I had received a sound, basic education. I had professional teachers, people who gave their hearts and souls to the children. They were rigorous, demanding, but they were fair. I know I

CHAPTER SEVEN

couldn't have done as well as I did at Central or later without this foundation.

"Our teachers took us to concerts sometimes; they encouraged reading contests, things like that, above and beyond the call of duty. It paid off. I especially remember Mrs. Bush, my junior high English teacher. She sensed my capabilities, my obsession with reading, and spurred me on."

Sybil's mother, who taught elementary school in Little Rock, kept taking summer classes, and eventually completed her master's degree at the University of Arkansas.

"We had a strong tradition of education in our family," Lorraine Jordan said. "There was always the expectation that Sybil would go on through high school and into college. We never doubted it."

"The family was involved in lots of community and church activities," Sybil recalled. At 17, Sybil was a "candy striper," doing hospital volunteer work. "That's the kind of job where you learn firsthand about sacrifices and priorities," she pointed out. "My brother and I often found ourselves in problem-solving situations; we used to have lively family discussions about almost everything under the sun. All this conditioned us for later in life when we faced tough situations." Central High was the first of those tough situations, but it wasn't the last.

"We took family trips every summer," Lorraine Jordan said. "I'm a great baseball fan, and we used to take everyone on the road to Milwaukee and Chicago and St. Louis to follow the Brooklyn Dodgers when they made their western swing. We went to all the games, but we would visit the zoos and museums in the cities, too. We got to know Jackie Robinson and Roy Campanella. They were our heroes in those days." (In 1947 Robinson had been the first black baseball player to break the color barrier in the major leagues and had a remarkable career.) Sybil also became an inveterate sports fan; later in life she avidly followed college basketball and found ways to attend some of the NCAA's Final Four tournaments.

SYBIL JORDAN STEVENSON

As lifelong residents of the Capitol Hill neighborhood, all the Jordans watched with anxiety and concern as the situation at Central High crystallized in the summer of 1957. Sybil was moving through her final years at Dunbar Junior High as the legal and figurative battle lines were drawn.

The turbulent events of the next two years changed the spirit and character of Central High, perhaps forever. While the nation and much of the world watched and listened, the school underwent a baptism by fire, oath, threat, and innuendo, especially for the nine young black students ("the Nine") who survived the 1957–58 years. They helped establish a vital beachhead for all those who would follow.

As the cooling-off period ended and the schools prepared to open at the beginning of the fall term of 1959, Sybil applied to enter Central High, aided by Daisy Bates (a prominent publisher and NAACP leader) and NAACP lawyers. There was a three-week delay, but she was finally admitted and began the daily ritual of being driven to school under the watchful eye of local police and the National Guard troops who remained on duty.

"Despite everything," Sybil said, "I followed a regular college preparatory course—algebra, geometry, biology, English, and social studies. But I was always alone, isolated.

"Inside the classrooms, it wasn't so bad. In the corridors, rest rooms, and cafeteria, it was something else.

"My teachers were wonderful, though. They saw that I was bright and worked hard, and they accepted me as a good student, no matter what their personal problems might have been. They were good teachers, professionals. They demanded attention and respect. When that classroom door was closed, they took no stuff. But out in the hallway they couldn't protect you. I was terrorized sometimes, I was pushed around, I was kicked in the shins." She still has a scar on one leg.

"But in some ways, the psychological part was the hardest to take, the hardest for a teenager to understand. It was

CHAPTER SEVEN

devastating. I kept wondering why this 'nonpersonal' thing was happening to me. I was lonely, I was treated as if I had a strange disease, and I guess I did: the disease of color. For the first time in my life, it was painfully clear to me that no one wanted to be with me, nor I with them. I felt so vulnerable."

From her executive office high above the well-kept grounds of GTE, Sybil Stevenson looked back with both candor and compassion at her days at Central High.

"Later on, 20 years later, at a high school reunion, many of my old classmates came up to tell me how badly they felt about what had happened. More than once the principal himself told me he was sorry but state rules didn't permit 'Negroes' to participate in clubs, parties, sporting events ... I had absolutely no social life. Nothing.

"But I learned, I developed a real siege mentality, I survived. And I had a great deal of help from my parents and from others, people in the church.

"My parents were always concerned about my safety ... we drove to school in a car pool. Plainclothes police sat across from our house every day. There were phone threats, insults. My folks kept up our strength, they said 'This too shall pass,' and 'There's a reason for all this. Be the best person you can, hold your head up!' The church, Bethel African Methodist Episcopal, played a vital role. We had faith in God's will, in His support. It all helped. We came through."

In her book, *Crisis at Central High School*, Elizabeth Huckaby wrote movingly about the strife in Little Rock during that period. She re-created the bitterness, danger, and fear that teachers and students lived through; all of the incidents of physical and psychological violence, the hot soup poured down girls' necks, the graffiti on restroom mirrors, the anonymous phone calls and crudely written letters.

Mrs. Huckaby, who was one of Sybil's teachers, served as vice principal for girls and taught English for 30 years.

She capsulized in a single incident the attitude of most teachers at Central back then. A white student had stuck his head in her classroom one day and yelled: "Are you going to let those niggers stay?" To which Mrs. Huckaby had replied, "Boy, this is a *school*!"

Throughout those difficult times, Sybil became acquainted with members of the American Friends Committee that had come to work in Little Rock. She participated in some of their work-camp activities and traveled to Washington, D.C., with them to see President John F. Kennedy's inauguration on a wintry day in 1961.

As part of their longstanding mission, the Quakers had worked to create bonds of friendship and understanding between blacks and whites in Little Rock, and the Jordans had responded to their philosophy. Sybil especially remembers Thelma Babbitt, who reached out to help her and who was one of those responsible for her interest in the possibility of attending Earlham College in Richmond, Indiana, a Quaker institution.

As the time approached for college applications, Sybil knew that she wanted to leave Arkansas and get away from the tensions of Little Rock. Her first choices were Bryn Mawr in Pennsylvania, Wheaton in Massachusetts, and Washington University in St. Louis. Earlham had also been highly recommended to her by people at the National Scholarship Service and Fund for Negro Students (NSSFNS); there was, too, the chance of a scholarship for her.

The counselors at Central High gave Sybil professional advice and helped in her planning for the move to college. But she sensed an underlying animosity and suspicion on the part of at least one teacher. "Sybil was an honor student," her mother recalled. "She had all A's except for one B in Spanish, and that kept her from having a perfect record. Her Spanish teacher wouldn't give her an A despite the fact that she was excellent in the subject. She had even had a private

CHAPTER SEVEN

tutor to help her perfect her accent. Later on at Earlham she was placed in advanced Spanish classes because of her ability. The teacher at Central was just spiteful, I guess."

Nevertheless, Sybil ranked about sixtieth in a class of over 500, close to the top 10 percent. She received a conditional acceptance at Bryn Mawr because her record was a little weak in science courses. "I was leaning toward one of the Seven Sisters because of their competitive nature," Sybil said, "but my parents weren't so sure I was ready for a place like that."

The scholarship from National Scholarship Service and Fund for Negro Students came through, Earlham offered some more aid, and "I had a work-study grant that paid a share of my tuition," Sybil added. "My folks still had to make up the difference in costs, and that was a real sacrifice for them. But they were prepared for it, and I was on my way."

The Jordans packed up the family car and all made the long drive to Indiana to take Sybil to Earlham. "It was hard to leave her," her mother said, "but she had been away from home before, and we knew she was on the right road."

"The minute I stepped out of the car and someone came up to me and said, 'Hi, Sybil Jordan, welcome!' I knew it was the right place," Sybil recalled. "Earlham was a really neat place from the start—lots of people from the Midwest, some from the Eastern prep schools like Sidwell Friends and Mount Herman—a mix of all kinds, black and white. I was not an unusual case to them—not too many even knew about things at Little Rock—and the transition was easier than I had expected. The spirit of the Friends was immediately apparent."

Earlham is a small, coeducational liberal arts college of about 1,000 students, founded by the Quakers. It is 70 miles east of Indianapolis, almost on the Ohio border, a quiet place. Costs are relatively high, but many students—then and now—pay their way through a combination of grants, loans, and work-study.

Later, Sybil wrote about her freshman experience at the college. "My appreciation for the warmth at Earlham stemmed from my need to be in a supportive environment after the trauma of integrating Central High. It was a community where differences were not just tolerated; where individual worth was respected; where whole new worlds were open to be explored."

Yet things were not all sweetness and light. "I struggled as a student. Academically, it was difficult. And there was an emerging social awareness that I had to cope with. I learned that Pappagallo shoes and Villager skirts were far more fashionable than the clothes I owned. But my roommates and faculty families helped ease me through transitions like this and I began to build confidence.

"My earlier experiences with the Quaker philosophy had been of immense help as I moved on. My flexibility, which grew out of the Little Rock trials, kept me loose and off the defensive. I look back on my Earlham years with great fondness and affection. Having been there made a real difference in my life. I had been tested and proved worthy. I strove to be excellent."

As part of her college experience, Sybil won an Experiment in International Living Scholarship and traveled to Japan in 1963 to live for two months with a Japanese family. Later, she renewed this friendship on another trip to the Orient.

On graduation weekend at Earlham, Sybil Jordan received her degree with a major in English literature, and married one of her college classmates, John Stevenson, who had won a Woodrow Wilson Fellowship and was going to study at the University of Chicago.

"While I was at Earlham, I didn't have the foggiest clue as to what I would do with the rest of my life," Sybil said.

CHAPTER SEVEN

"I considered the idea of going into health education, but John had not been accepted at Berkeley or Columbia, which were the two places with health education programs. So we went together to Chicago, and I took an interim job working for the Social Security Administration.

"During that year I realized I didn't want to spend the rest of my life doing that, so I applied for a fellowship and began a master's degree program in education at the University of Chicago.

"The Hyde Park environment was marvelous—interesting and stimulating. I got my master's and taught in the Louis Champlain Elementary School for a year before continuing graduate studies...."

By that time five years had elapsed and it became apparent that the marriage would not work out. Sybil and John Stevenson decided to go their own ways, and after an amicable separation, she left Chicago and moved to the New York area in 1971. Her goal at that point was to continue her graduate studies at Columbia University.

"However, I was fortunate enough to land a job at Iona College, in their Higher Education Opportunity Program," Sybil recalled. "That gave me another entirely different perspective on education and on life, and I was obliged to make a whole new series of adjustments there."

Located in New Rochelle, just outside New York City, Iona is an undergraduate college of about 6,000 students, mainly commuters, with some master's degree programs and a business school. The college did not admit women until 1969, when the Vatican granted a special exception; now the ratio of women to men is about 45 to 55.

Essentially, Sybil's job was to develop and expand educational support services for disadvantaged students at Iona, but she soon realized that the challenges involved much more than that. "To begin with, I was the first woman administrator there, at a historically Catholic institution [founded in

1940 by the Irish Christian Brothers]. It was a very male-dominated place. Both sides had adjustments to make."

"It's important to know our heritage and mission," Brother Francis Offer noted. As a faculty member and director of admissions for over two decades, he became a close friend of Sybil Stevenson. "We were founded to teach the poor, and, of course, that meshed closely with Sybil's first assignments. We have many first-generation college students even today, many with Italian, Irish, and Spanish surnames.

"Sybil first came to us as an intern during her graduate work at the University of Chicago. When a vacancy occurred in our HEOP program, Brother Driscoll, the president, asked her to stay on full time.

"HEOP had started at Iona in 1966 with only 10 students a year, but now it has grown to include more than 80, and Sybil deserves much of the credit for helping build and extend the program."

"As I began to settle in," Sybil recalled, "it was a surprise to me that I was dealing with a whole new group here—tough inner-city kids who somehow found me totally out of step with their needs and desires. I think they really disliked me at the beginning. They were suspicious of me; I worked too closely with whites; I spoke properly; and there was even some doubt in their minds if I was really black, or black enough, anyway. This all came as something of a shock to me after all I had been through.

"There I was at the tender age of 27 or 28, just 5 years out of college, only 10 years away from the scene at Little Rock, but to them I was the enemy.

"Although I was outraged, I challenged them back. I persevered. I knew I faced a real challenge and that somehow I had to build bridges back to these young people. Little by little, I came to understand that they all had their own special problems, reflecting their private hassles at home, hang-ups at school, bad neighborhoods, and so on. They came to

CHAPTER SEVEN

learn that I cared, and while I was tough-minded, I was fair. I helped them accomplish their goals. I told them outright, 'You don't have to like me, but *use* me; we can get it done together.' They got the idea."

Brother Offer agreed. "Sybil ran a tight ship. She demanded rigor, high standards, and discipline. Some resisted, but eventually almost all of the HEOP students came to respect her, and later in life a number returned to the college to visit."

"I told the students that I would ask a lot, but if they were serious about getting a degree, about surviving at Iona and moving on, I would help them," Sybil said. "We all moved ahead together."

During her five years at HEOP, she supervised a staff of four, wrote funding proposals, managed a budget of about $300,000 yearly, produced recruiting materials, and carried out a range of activities related to community organizations and agencies.

In recognition of her administrative skills and diplomacy, the college promoted her to serve as an assistant to Charles O'Donnell, dean of the School of Arts and Sciences. Her new responsibilities included working on the formulation of academic policy, curriculum development, financial administration, and coordination of special programs.

"Sybil became a vital part of the administration," Brother Offer said. "She helped us through some changes in personnel and provided important continuity. She was also well accepted by *both* faculty and administration, not a common occurrence, and certainly one key to her success at Iona. She was a real guiding light in all areas where academic problems arose."

By 1978 Sybil had been named assistant dean of the School of Arts and Sciences and had also begun to think again about continuing her studies at Columbia University, with the goal of first completing a master's degree in higher education administration and then moving on toward her doctorate.

"I feel sure Sybil will always maintain her ties with higher education," Brother Offer said. "I think her work now with GTE is fine experience, and perhaps a logical transition for her at this point in time. But she has much of the academician in her. She's a teacher at heart, by instinct perhaps. That's where her roots are."

Sybil's outside activities continued while she moved up in the hierarchy at Iona. In 1976 she served as reader and evaluator for the HEOP program for the state of New York in Albany. That year she was also on the faculty of a special New York State summer workshop for financial-aid administration, and in 1980 she finally made her connection with Bryn Mawr College by taking a temporary job there as assistant director of the Summer Institute for Women in Academic Administration.

"This was a pivotal experience for me," she remembered. "First, because I got to be at Bryn Mawr, to live there, to see what it was like. And second, it helped me to make the decision to concentrate seriously on graduate school. As I look back now, I was happy to go to Bryn Mawr as an adult, and yet pleased that I hadn't gone there as a young student. It would have been quite too much for me . . . my parents were right, as usual."

In early 1985 the opportunity came to join GTE. It was a singular, and in some ways frightening prospect, moving out of the familiar academic world after more than a dozen exciting and rewarding years, and into the relatively unknown atmosphere of one of the top Fortune 500 corporations.

"There was great appeal for me," Sybil said "and also some anxiety, but I knew of GTE's reputation and their determination to carry on and extend their social responsibilities. I felt this gave me a chance to move onto the

CHAPTER SEVEN

national stage, and perhaps play my own role in affecting the future."

Looking back at Iona, Sybil remembered that "those were good years, sometimes difficult, but always interesting, always stimulating." She received several honors during her time at the college. In 1976 she was picked as one of the Outstanding Young Women of America. In 1979 the New Rochelle branch of the NAACP honored her for her achievements in education, and not long after she joined GTE, Iona College named her as its Woman of Achievement for 1986, noting in the citation that she was so honored because she had overcome major obstacles to achieve success in the fields of education and business.

As she made the transition to GTE, Sybil continued to work on her Ph.D. at Teachers College at Columbia, focusing on the important connections between higher education and business. With the encouragement of Teachers College president Lawrence Cremin, she continued her studies exploring the interdependence of the two worlds. As she put it, "I wanted another career option so I could use my educational background in a different setting. A number of colleges and corporations are now developing these concepts, looking at new ways to parlay old strengths, teaching backgrounds, into useful roles in business and industry.

"Through their corporate contributions program, GTE is carrying on a philanthropic tradition begun many years ago by people like the Rockefellers and the Fords, Andrew Carnegie, Alfred Sloan, and others who decided to use their profits to benefit society," Sybil commented. "GTE programs include gifts in a number of fields: health, human services, civic leadership, and those I concentrate on, education and culture. Our contributions presently reach over two dozen colleges and universities, and we tend to concentrate on areas of particular interest to the corporation: business administration, engineering, and computer science, for example."

Her other responsibilities include supervising GTE efforts in precollege math and science education, special grants addressing critical national issues in higher education, and the new GTE Foundation Lectureships in Science, Technology, and Human Values.

From time to time Sybil Jordan Stevenson thinks back to the difficult days when she first walked with pride and apprehension up the steps of Central High School.

"A lot has happened since then," she mused, "some very positive and encouraging things, some perplexing and even discouraging." She is keenly aware of the decline in black enrollment in colleges and universities since its peak in the 1970s, reflecting government cuts in funds for financial aid, support services, and counseling.

She has started to wonder if perhaps a new generation of Americans, black and white, have not already begun to forget the gauntlet that she and a handful of other black teenagers dared to take up in Little Rock, and then in Selma and Montgomery. History has a way of absorbing and blotting out the details, the special acts of personal courage and sacrifice that make causes succeed and give substance to principles of law and reason.

The courageous behavior of "the Nine" and Sybil Jordan Stevenson at Central High School set important legal and personal precedents. The confrontation there did not take place simply to protect a few black students, but to protect an idea; it was not a question of race, but one of principle.

Not long ago, Sybil joined several hundred others in Little Rock for a reunion of their high school class. "It was interesting," she said, "and quite a revelation, too. It's the first one I ever attended. I wasn't even invited before this.

"They had a nice dinner at the 4-H facility outside town, with dancing and a program—all the trappings of a reunion. My parents went with me, and people couldn't have been nicer to us. Many came up to me to say how glad they were

CHAPTER SEVEN

that I had come, and how sorry they were about my treatment in school, how cruel people had been. I even got an award for being 'one of the best educated.'

"The president of our senior class, who had never spoken to me in all those years at school, sat with us at dinner. But I don't think he—or anyone—particularly felt remorse so much as they did regret. Things are changing in Little Rock, I guess. I'm hopeful. I've always been a positive and optimistic person."

If Sybil and the others had not led the way, it is unlikely that in the 1980s we would have black mayors in Los Angeles and Philadelphia and Detroit. There might be far fewer black athletes starring in the NBA and the NFL, and it seems doubtful that TV's number-one show would feature the black family of a successful physician whose daughter goes to Princeton. Nor would anyone have suspected in 1960 that in a little over two decades there would be a serious black candidate for the presidency of the United States.

Now, after a quarter century, the big stone high school looks much the same. From identical poles on the front lawn, the U.S. and Arkansas State flags fly quietly and equitably in the faint breeze. Half of the students are black, and so is a third of the faculty. There have been two black principals in recent years. Graduates still win their fair share of honors and National Merit Scholarships and move on to colleges and universities. And, some say, late in the afternoon, after the cleanup crews have swept through the lofty corridors and the building stands empty, the echoes return: the shouts and screams of the crowd outside; the steadfast voices of the teachers; the purposeful sounds of hundreds of students on their way to class, on their way to learn the lessons still ahead.

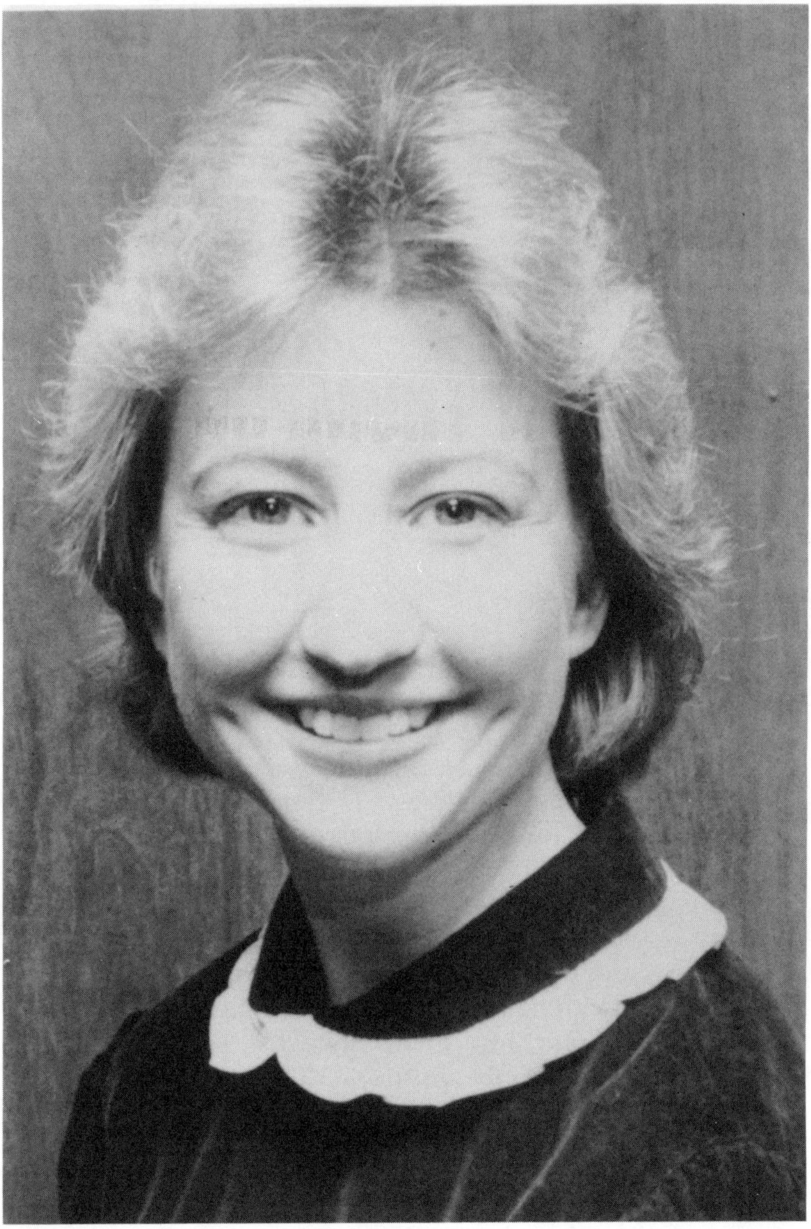

Chapter 8

CAROLYN THOMPSON

For more than 40 years, the oil well known as Petunia #1, which stands at the steps of the state capitol in Oklahoma City, faithfully pumped some 600 barrels of oil per day, providing the state with more than a million dollars in royalties and taxes. Now, Petunia has gone dry, and its mile-deep well beneath the capitol building has been capped, though the spidery derrick remains in place.

It was with a sense of irony that on a mild, overcast Tuesday, January 6, 1987, the newly elected members of the forty-first legislature filed past Petunia's skeletal remains, up the steps of the Indiana limestone building, between the ornate Corinthian columns, and into their chambers for the opening session. Their minds were focused on ways and means to cope with the drastic worldwide drop in oil prices and revenues that had shaken the Southwest, affecting businesses, schools, and personal lives.

These men and women are by history and tradition pioneers; their parents and grandparents survived frontier

CHAPTER EIGHT

wars and Dust Bowl depressions. They have the toughness and resilience of pathfinders and Plains Indians, and they have full faith in their state motto: *Labor Omnia Vincit*, labor conquers everything.

This young, ambitious, and highly trained group of 149 representatives and senators, public servants tuned to the times, were prepared to take positive action for change. There were only 13 women among them, 6 in the Senate and 7 in the House, and one, Carolyn Thompson from Norman, had won reelection to her second term by a resounding 70 percent of the vote.

At age 30, slender, 5'4", with blonde hair and greenish eyes, she is one of the youngest women ever to serve in the House. She has already demonstrated her energy and leadership on several committees, and through the introduction of legislation that generated a sweeping review of higher education throughout the state.

She is intensely proud of her family's heritage and their contributions to the state. When her great-grandparents arrived from Germany in the nineteenth century, Oklahoma was still a territory, and they opened Norman's first shoe store (which is still in business).

She is also keenly aware of her own special responsibilities as one of the few women in positions of leadership in this legislature. On the day of the opening session she moved easily among the other members of the House as they exchanged greetings and handshakes and took their assigned seats in the high-backed black leather chairs that are arranged in nine precise rows facing the rostrum. By her reelection, she had gained seniority and moved forward two rows from her back-bench position.

In the gallery of the pale green and gold room, her mother, father, sisters, and brothers looked down with pride as the gavel sounded just after noon and the new governor, Henry Bellmon, gave his State of the State address. Later Carolyn received an unusual assignment for a sophomore legislator: she was asked to introduce the speaker of the House, Jim Barker, and to nominate him for another term as speaker.

There was concern and anxiety in the legislature, but there was also a feeling of determination and innovation as the brief opening session got under way. Oklahoma license plates declare that "Oklahoma is OK" and Carolyn Thompson seems the embodiment of that spirit of vigor and confidence. As she said during her 1984 election campaign, "I have told hundreds of Norman High School students that government should never be a spectator sport. I firmly believe it. I cannot and will not sit idly by and watch others turn out the lights on Oklahoma's future."

A native of Norman, whose parents and grandparents have deep roots in the community, she went through the elementary grades at St. Joseph's parochial school and finished in the public schools. She graduated from the University of Oklahoma with an A.B. degree in history in 1979 and returned to Norman High that same year to teach government while she continued her graduate studies.

Throughout her twin careers thus far, she has remained fascinated and disturbed by the question of why more Americans aren't involved in politics, why they are not better informed and more active in campaigns and in exercising their precious right to vote. "People in many countries around the world would make any sacrifice—give their lives—for the rights and privileges that many of our people disregard or neglect," she observed when talking about the closely interwoven threads of her own political and educational life.

It's hard for Carolyn to understand inactivity and detachment. She herself is a model of involvement, and through much of her life she has been a joiner, a participant, a doer. "I always thought it was important to have a broad range of experience as you grow up and go through school," she said. "Not just to be doing things, but to help you understand the

CHAPTER EIGHT

interests and abilities of a variety of people, what's on their minds. Maybe that's why I have done well in the legislature. I'm a good listener. I can identify with people's concerns and problems, from the university's construction budget to the needs of mental-health programs or retail grocers in Norman."

During one rainy week in late February, after the 1987 session was well under way, she took time out between floor votes, caucuses, research, and civic commitments to discuss her life, her current responsibilities, and her goals. In the course of one typical (if not average) 14-hour workday, she talked in her car, on the run, at lunch and dinner, and in the small but comfortable quarters that she shares with six other representatives on the third floor of the capitol.

The tangible rewards for this kind of commitment are not overwhelming. State representatives and senators receive $20,000 for the five or six months that the legislature is in session. That's about what the average teacher makes in Oklahoma.

From the first of the year until early June, Carolyn leads a busy life in the fast lane, and spends many hours in her white Mustang, shuttling between Oklahoma City and Norman on a 40-mile stretch of Interstate 35.

How do the days go? Consider Tuesday, February 24. "I started today with a 7:30 a.m. working breakfast at the Faculty House of the School of Medicine here in town," Carolyn said. "Then about 9:30 I met with Speaker Jim Barker to talk about appropriations and budget. By 11 a.m. I was in another meeting at the capitol, and at noon I went to an award luncheon. There were a couple of roll calls in the afternoon, and later on, more committee meetings."

She paused to look at her calendar. Her private office is cozy (some might say cramped), maybe 10-feet square, and brightly lit by overhead fluorescent panels. There's a beige Danish modern sofa and a couple of side chairs. Her desk is neat, with piles of papers and bills stacked carefully. The walls are decorated with a framed copy of her 1986 election certificate, a replica of the Declaration of Independence, a Norman Rockwell calendar, and a humorous poster from Colonial Williamsburg. On that particular Tuesday she was wearing a simple dark green dress with a white Puritan collar and lace cuffs.

"Around four," she continued, "we had a special meeting of the Economic Development Committee and then there was one I really liked, a presentation of the Tinker Air Force Base Award to Frank Miller, who happens to be my father. He has worked as a civilian engineer at Tinker for about 30 years now and I was proud of that recognition of him.

"A little later, the Oklahoma Legislative Arts group met, and by 5:30 p.m. or so I was ready for a short break. I took maybe a half-hour to go to my apartment, a temporary home away from home, shower, change clothes—and gears—and head for the fairgrounds to take part in the annual barbecue and hoedown of the Oklahoma Education Association. Being a teacher, I could hardly miss that one. It seemed like hundreds of my friends were there; it was like old home week. The food was pretty good, too—barbecue, potato salad, coleslaw, and all the trimmings. I guess I got home about 10 p.m. and found time and strength for reading a few background papers for the next day. I slept pretty well," she concluded with a smile.

It is that kind of stamina and flexibility that has earned Carolyn Thompson the respect of many of the legislators she works with in the House. State Senator Stratton Taylor from the Claremore-Tulsa area remarked at her ability to serve all constituencies. "She must represent diverse publics in Norman," he noted. "Aside from the university, there is a children's hospital, a VA facility, and a range of businesses and industries. She must understand the needs of the whole spectrum and she does, with sensitivity.

"You must remember, too," he added, "that when she first ran in '84 she was only 27 years old, and she beat a well-

CHAPTER EIGHT

known and experienced Republican woman, winning some 60 percent of the vote. How did she do it? By hard work and optimism, I guess. And by doing her homework. She knocked on every door in Norman. They all like her down there. They like her positive outlook. She has the ethics of a Mahatma Gandhi, and she can deliver the goods."

Carolyn may have learned some of her discipline and commitment from the teachers at St. Joseph's elementary school which she attended through the fifth grade. "The nuns still wore the old black robes then," she recalled. "We went to mass every morning and prayed. We had religion classes, too, but I never studied Latin. There was a real respect for learning at St. Joe's and I got a good foundation there. But when it closed, I moved on to public schools. I always enjoyed school, learning new things."

"She just seemed to start out mature," her mother, Jo Anne Miller, said. "She was quiet at home, but always competitive and involved in many things on the outside. She had lots of energy and initiative, but so did all the children. Everyone studied music, and most of them were pretty good; Carolyn and her sister Donna played in the band at high school and later at the university. We went to lots of concerts and recitals while they were growing up."

Carolyn mentioned that her mother was musically talented and that everyone in the family took up at least one instrument. "I studied piano for a dozen years or more and I thought of making it a career at one point," she said. "But I moved on to other things. I did lots of reading as a kid. I won some awards for it. I read everything I could get my hands on. There was never any question that I would go on to college. I never thought about any other possibility, and my parents were fully supportive, even though there were six of us in the family. We knew we would have to watch our dollars and that we'd have to work to help pay our way."

"We paid for their books and tuition," Jo Anne Miller said, "and we took out student loans. But they all worked in high school and college. Carolyn had a job at a local cafeteria and she did baby-sitting, too. In college she worked at the campus jewelry store. But she never neglected her academic work and she carried a full load every semester."

"We were a close-knit family," Frank Miller recalled. "We still are. There's a real feeling of interdependence, if you will. We feel strongly that we are all part of this town, this community, just as our parents were."

He attended Norman High School and the University of Oklahoma, where he received a degree in aeronautical engineering, and later an M.A. in business administration. Once an Eagle scout himself, Miller served for eight years as a scoutmaster in town.

"All our children have been academically oriented. Two daughters and a son graduated from the university, and one son is a senior in engineering there now. Another son is on duty with the U.S. Air Force in San Antonio, Texas.

"Talk about family roots," Miller said, "ours go way back. Carolyn's great-grandfather opened the first shoe shop in Norman, and it's still going—an uncle runs it now.

"In recent years I have combined my computer abilities with our interest in the family's genealogy. I've started an in-depth research effort to trace our roots, and so far I have about 5,000 entries stored on disks. That takes us through great-great grandparents.

"It is interesting, too, that Jo Anne and I were born in adjacent houses in Norman and went all through school together. It almost sounds like something from *Our Town*, doesn't it?" Through the years, Jo Anne Miller has worked, too, but as Carolyn noted, "She was a full-time mother, she was always there when we needed her."

The family cohesion carried over into vacations. Jo Anne Miller recalled that, "We took lots of family trips in the summers. We all piled into the station wagon and headed for places like Disneyland, Seattle, Washington, D.C., and, of course, Six Flags in Texas. That was a favorite."

CHAPTER EIGHT

"My parents stressed travel," Carolyn said. "We went together on lots of low-budget trips, packed lunches, stayed in places like Motel 6. They weren't luxury tours, but we all enjoyed them and saw a lot of the land. I feel it's important for families to do that together."

Carolyn moved briskly into Norman High School, following in the path of her parents and siblings. The school is a cluster of low, modern, red-brick buildings connected by open breezeways and bordered by wide stretches of lawn. The corridors and classrooms are well maintained and seem to reflect the general tone and spirit of the students. The enrollment is about 1,500, not greatly changed from the days in the 1970s when Carolyn was there. The school mirrors in many ways the town of 70,000 that encircles it.

Like State College, Pennsylvania, and Bloomington, Indiana, and a score of other university towns around the country, Norman's socioeconomic life focuses on and is nourished by the university. The pace and style of the community change with the seasons; in the fall, winter, and spring some 22,000 students are in residence; in the summer months the momentum slows. There is probably greater cultural diversity than in most other Oklahoma cities, more of a cosmopolitan feeling, and active interest in the arts and theater. As Carolyn noted, Norman has the youngest population and probably the best educated one in the state; recent figures indicate that about 68 percent of the people in her district have some college education.

"High school was fun for me," Carolyn said. "I kept up my reading, lots of history and biography. I didn't get into novels and fiction until later." Her early heroes included John F. Kennedy and Martin Luther King, Jr., and she also developed a keen appreciation of the contributions of Franklin, Jefferson, and Hamilton.

"We never watched much TV. We just didn't seem to have time for it. I was in the band, and involved in lots of church activities, too. My grades were good enough in the college-preparatory subjects, and I felt sure that I would move on to OU—that's the regular expectation in Norman. We didn't really have very good counseling in those days, but I think it is better now. We had only three counselors for something like 1,500 students, and you had to make an appointment weeks in advance. So we did a lot of self-guidance and peer counseling."

"Carolyn did well in high school," her mother remembered. "She was busy in the band, and in Girl's State, and other things, but she kept her perspective. She didn't become a grind. And in our family, we had another incentive, too. All the kids had to keep at least 3.0 average if they wanted to have a driver's license and a chance to use the car. That was no problem for Carolyn. She maintained a good overall average, though I do recall she was a little weak in science and math."

In the 1975 yearbook Carolyn appears in several pictures sporting a modified pageboy and sometimes a miniskirt. Local civic groups selected her for the "outstanding student award."

As she moved toward the university, Carolyn's interest in government and teaching continued. Some of her strongest encouragement and inspiration came from Mrs. Viola Smith, a teacher of government at Norman High. Their relationship extended through Carolyn's collegiate years and on into her legislative career.

"There is no greater reward for a teacher than to see one of her best students succeed," Viola Smith once wrote. "I have had the unique opportunity to observe Carolyn as a student, student teacher, and colleague. She approaches each task with a determination and skill that have earned her the respect of students, parents, and fellow teachers alike."

Mrs. Smith postponed her own retirement to help Carolyn in her first campaign for the House, and later, not long

CHAPTER EIGHT

before her death, Viola was invited to visit the legislature where she received special recognition on the floor for her long career in teaching.

Some of Carolyn's high school teachers had an intuitive feeling that she would follow a teaching career, and they were not surprised to see her join them on the faculty at Norman High. Jim Power, who teaches American literature, said, "She was animated and involved. She was always an excellent communicator. Her writing and thinking were clear and logical, forceful and persuasive."

In the fall of 1975 Carolyn entered the University of Oklahoma and was quickly caught up in the activities of the bustling campus. While it is recognized as one of the quality academic institutions of the Southwest, the university has attracted national attention and identity as a major football power. Every fall millions of TV viewers watch the Sooners win conference championships and, frequently, national titles, usually in the Orange Bowl. Though she spent a lot of time attending classes and studying in the red-brick library allegedly described by architect Frank Lloyd Wright as "Cherokee Gothic," Carolyn devoted many long hours every fall to band practice, and became an integral part of the Saturday spectacle. She still remembers those crisp autumn afternoons when nearly 70,000 fans filled the huge stadium, and particularly the tense moments of hushed expectancy just before the football game as the band assembled in the tunnel to make its entrance.

When the teams had finished their warm-ups they would stand quietly alongside the benches, dancing nervously in place, fidgeting with their helmets. Then, upon the conductor's signal, the band would explode into action with the sharp, brassy sounds of (naturally) "Oklahoma!" and surge onto the field in their bright red-and-white uniforms.

Nearly 300 strong, they stepped out smartly in perfect unison, prancing across the astroturf. The crowd roared its approval and joined in singing. At one end of a marching row, her uniform cap aligned perfectly, eyes straight ahead, white leggings spotless, Carolyn moved as one with the band, elbows pointed, adding the notes of her piccolo to the total musical impact that echoed around the packed stadium.

"Being in the band was only a part of my college experience," Carolyn said, "but it was a memorable part, and I think that in any large institution like OU students tend to identify with and remember the pleasant times, the periods they spent following their special interests. The academic courses are vital, the preparation for jobs and careers, but there's more to a university. Whether you are in the band or on the student newspaper or in theater, these things all come together to make up the incomparable experiences of a liberal education. Maybe that's why I feel so strongly about and take such pride in having the university in my district and carrying the responsibility for representing it in Oklahoma City."

One of Carolyn's fellow band members was Richard Thompson, a percussionist who planned to be a professional musician. They became close friends and in 1977, when Carolyn was 20, they were married. But as they moved toward graduation, both recognized that they were headed for clearly diverging careers and lifestyles. A year after their marriage they separated—on good terms and by mutual consent.

Richard traveled to New York following their divorce and is now a successful jazz musician there. Carolyn concentrated on completing her history degree and teacher preparation activities. In the fall of 1979, just four years after graduation from Norman High School, she returned to join the faculty there. In the course of the next five years she distinguished herself as a teacher of psychology and history, and particularly in a course on U.S. government that she taught to college-bound seniors.

One of her close friends and fellow teachers in those days, Donna Hamilton, talked about Carolyn's special abilities "to listen, to relate to young people. She had a keen personal

CHAPTER EIGHT

interest in making the course interesting and timely. She used current news stories, magazines, and trips to the state capital and to Washington. She stimulated the kids, she made them realize they were a vital part of the government, not just bystanders."

Hamilton, who was herself voted Teacher of the Year by the Oklahoma Education Association, said that Carolyn "brought government to life, partly through her own understanding and conviction of the power and durability of our system. It's no wonder she has become a legislator, it's almost in her blood."

Jo Anne Miller recalled her daughter's dedication. "I know she loved her teaching, it seemed to come naturally to her. She always made that extra effort in preparation. She took her classes to visit the university, to civic meetings, and to the city council here in town. She seemed to draw energy from her students; they sustained her."

The University of Oklahoma's vice-provost for instructional services, Jerry Weber, reflected on his son's experience in Carolyn's classes at Norman High. "The kids developed a real sense of pride in their work with her—for her—and the remarkable thing is that while they respected her discipline and demanding standards, they also liked her style and felt real friendship for her. My son still counts her as a good friend today."

J. R. Morris, retired provost of the university and now regents professor, recalled Carolyn's unique skills in both teaching and campaigning. "She was unshockable. Unflappable. She could cope with any situation, in the classroom or on the campaign trail. I remember when she was teaching at Norman High School and brought her students up here to visit. Like their teacher, they were bright, sophisticated, and well prepared. She had an excellent reputation around the state as a superior teacher. She hasn't changed, and she applies those abilities in the legislature now."

Asked why she was such a good teacher, Carolyn responded: "Probably because I was young. But also because I demanded a lot. Students respect that. They worked hard, they met all my challenges. Mine was an elective course, so they were for the most part highly motivated. I learned a lot from them, too, as any good teacher does. Many of them still keep in touch and write to me."

As they put theory into practice in 1984, some of her former students at Norman High worked for her election. They testified that "government wasn't just memorizing dates and names with Carolyn Thompson as our teacher. She helped us understand how the system works and how each individual can play an important part ... she was always willing to stay late or come early if we needed extra help."

One of Carolyn's professors at OU, Russell Buhite, has said that "she represented a victory for those of us who want our best university students to go into teaching. She was an outstanding history and political science student at the university ... and while we will miss her in the classroom, we need our best working for us in the state legislature."

Even as she excelled in her teaching role at the high school, Carolyn was continuing to work on a graduate degree at the university, and in 1984 she began seriously to consider making her first run for public office. The concept of blending the best of the two worlds strongly appealed to her; perhaps it was almost inevitable.

She entered the 1984 campaign as her district's Democratic candidate for the state legislature with a broad but perhaps shallow base. She was, in many ways, an unknown, with little political experience. She had been active in a number of civic and professional groups, but her opponent was a widely respected and seasoned legislator in her early sixties.

Late in April 1984 Carolyn was selected in a national competition as one of 20 educators who would represent the United States at a U.S. Department of Education Fulbright seminar on ancient and modern Middle Eastern politics, his-

CHAPTER EIGHT

tory, and culture. A trip to Israel was included in the schedule. Carolyn faced the difficult dilemma head on. She regretfully turned down the Fulbright honor, and jumped energetically into the campaign. "She hit the ground running," her sister remembered, "and we were all behind her. It became a family campaign, too."

Jo Anne Miller commented, "We all worked hard on that first campaign. Carolyn was clearly the underdog, but we had faith; we canvassed neighborhoods, we stuffed and licked envelopes. We made up sweatshirts, each with a different motto. Mine said in large print 'Carolyn Thompson,' and below in smaller print, it said, 'I'm her Mom.' We staged lots of hot dog and apple pie cookouts as fund-raisers. And when it was all over, I remember we spent part of Christmas day addressing and mailing cards and notes of thanks to her supporters."

Another OU professor, Drew Kershen, said during the campaign, "Carolyn Thompson is one of those people who doesn't spend a lot of time talking about her commitments and values. She is too busy acting on them . . . she never does a project halfway. She demonstrated her commitment to this office by giving up the prestigious Fulbright opportunity in order to devote full time to the campaign. We need more people in public service with her honesty and integrity."

The slogan for her campaign was "One of our own . . . one of the best," and this seemed to ring true for the several groups from which she drew strength. One supporter said, "I have watched Carolyn grow from a teenager to a mature adult . . . you always know where she stands and why . . . I want a representative who will stand firm for the things we care about in Norman."

A businesswoman said, "She brings an enthusiastic and professional attitude to every project in which she participates . . . I know she will bring the same determination to her job as a representative."

The record shows that she won the 1984 election handily,

with some 60 percent of the vote, and in early 1985 she began to divide her life between family, social, and educational commitments in Norman and her new responsibilities in Oklahoma City as representative of District 44.

As a freshman legislator, Carolyn came well prepared to her job and eager to learn some of the practical details not always spelled out in the textbooks on government. Her sense of fairness, open personality, and positive attitude quickly won friends and allies. She was selected to serve on several committees that reflected her interests and concerns: education and higher education; economic development; state and federal relations; and mental health.

In addition to the daily demands of the legislature, she kept up her course work toward a master's degree in political science at the university. She began to take on state and national commitments to participate in educational and governmental organizations, and traveled to Washington, D.C., and New York with some regularity. In 1984, in recognition of her expanding civic and professional work, she was named Young Career Woman of the Year by the business and professional women's group in Norman, and was also designated as one of the Outstanding Young Women of America the same year.

The past few years have been difficult for Oklahoma. Oil revenues have continued to decline, which has directly affected most segments of the economy. An important part of Carolyn's job was to absorb and evaluate some of the complex implications of this problem. As she wrote in 1986, "Our state faces an uncertain economic future. Clearly, we need new job opportunities and economic diversification—we desperately need a strategically planned program for the twenty-first century. To accomplish such goals we will require increased capital formation and innovation and must increase linkages with our vocational-technical and higher education systems and organized assistance to business."

Because of her background in education, Carolyn realized

CHAPTER EIGHT

that her own most useful contributions might well come in that field, in helping the legislature and the public understand better the need for a comprehensive review and reappraisal of the state's educational strengths and weaknesses. Oklahoma remains very near the bottom in rankings of state support for higher education.

"This means a thorough study of the entire system," she wrote, "from kindergarten to graduate research, including the issues of funding, quality, duplication, accessibility, governance, and economic impact. And," she added, "I know these concerns are not popular with many state legislators, but I have never been afraid to take tough stands on unpopular issues."

As an editorial in the Norman *Transcript* commented in 1986, she kept extremely busy. "Few freshman state legislators have been as effective as Carolyn Thompson . . . a teacher by profession, she quickly established herself as an expert on education and its application to economic development . . . and although new legislators are expected to sit quietly on the back row for their first couple of years, Representative Thompson has already authored or coauthored legislation in several areas . . . she has earned statewide respect, and is already considered one of our outstanding lawmakers."

Clearly, it was the sponsorship of the special task force on higher education that gained her the greatest acclaim and attention. Through family, training, and experience, Carolyn had come to believe that education is, indeed, a key to the state's future. She once wrote: "It is an intergenerational compact that ensures a future Oklahoma of families and children dedicated to progress. We must invest in people, not just things . . . we must invest in our major resource—the minds of our children and the aspiration of our citizens."

The comprehensive task force study took shape over a period of many months, and was not released until early 1987. It proposed sweeping changes in the structure, governance, and funding of higher education in the state. Many of the state's legislators and educators consider it a major accomplishment. Senator Taylor called this report Carolyn's "greatest achievement in her first years" and went on to say that she had "generated a statewide debate on higher education; she put it on the public agenda, and dramatized the needs and problems. The findings and recommendations of the report are now under widespread and spirited discussion. Not everyone likes it, but television, the editorial pages, and the universities themselves are talking about the questions, and that's important."

J. R. Morris agreed. "Carolyn deserves great credit for this study. She was the principal author and participant in the task force, and this was a blue-ribbon group. I think that while the substance of the report is very important, the symbolism is even more important. We have serious problems in higher education, and now they have been brought out in the open for full discussion; they have become highly visible."

The University of Oklahoma's president, Frank Horton, added, "There's no doubt that education is a key concern of hers, and one of her real strengths. She has that unique ability to span the age spectrum in her legislative work. And she's always open to new ideas, trial balloons. She's accessible."

Like all members of the House, Carolyn had to begin thinking about reelection almost before she got settled into the routine of the job. But she was able to defer active planning and campaigning until the late summer and fall of 1986.

In a letter to her constituency she outlined some of her views and goals for a second term. "The goal that must sustain Norman's representative," she wrote, "is preservation of the unique community that we have developed. I will continue to be a leader in that fight in the next legislature.

"I believe that at stake is our ability to attract and retain business, the creation of a stable fiscal base, and establishment and support of a comprehensive quality educational system.

CHAPTER EIGHT

"My first term taught me that reform often gets more talk than action . . . and it has been important to me to have successfully passed legislation in all areas of my committee work."

She reasserted her faith in the centrality of education. "Education is no longer only for our early years. Education for jobs that utilize new technology is a key to increasing our productivity and enhancing prosperity. . . . We must make additional educational opportunities available throughout our adult lives to maintain and continue improving our standard of living."

Carolyn knew that she would once again face an older, more experienced opponent, a local lawyer and Vietnam veteran. She knew the cold statistics that every two years about one-fourth of the incumbents lose their seats for various reasons, so she embarked on another vigorous campaign. This time her support had broadened and deepened. Her many civic and professional associations (among them the League of Women Voters, Cleveland County Democrat Women's Club, the Norman Chamber of Commerce, St. Thomas More, and the American Association of University Women) provided both funding and votes. Her record was an important factor. She was an incumbent who had demonstrated ability and visibility—and results.

During October, in the midst of her campaign efforts, Carolyn took a break to fly to New York and participate in a special program at the College Board's National Forum. On a Sunday morning, an hour or two before her program began, she relaxed in a small conference room at the Waldorf-Astoria hotel and continued her reflections on the progress of her dual career as educator and legislator. She looked bright and scrubbed, as though she had just stepped off the OU campus, although she had been out until well after midnight watching one of the critical World Series games between the New York Mets and the Boston Red Sox. How could she possibly have gotten tickets? "We took a positive approach," she reported. "My friend and I just rode out to Shea Stadium on the subway and bought a ticket. No problem. It was a great game!"

Later in the day she joined a panel of experts to discuss state and national issues in education. Presiding and delivering the keynote speech was the governor of New Jersey, Thomas Kean. Others on the panel included Frank Newman, president of the Education Commission of the States, Kenneth Ashworth, state commissioner for higher education in Texas, and Gordon Ambach, commissioner of education for New York State. There were about a thousand high school and college teachers and administrators from around the country in the audience.

When Carolyn's turn came to respond to Kean's remarks, she spoke cogently about the need for more focus on continuing education and better ways to include an aging population in the system, to accommodate older learners. She had the facts in hand, urged educators to speak out, reach out, be more involved in community groups and agencies, in government. She chose her words carefully and kept to the issues without wandering. There was never any uncertainty or groping for words, no need to fall back on the universal connector, "you know." It was a first-rate presentation, and she returned to Oklahoma reassured by the warm reception she had received from this national audience.

The 1986 election went well. Carolyn conducted an effective campaign; the family pitched in again, as did many new friends and allies. Her solid record of achievement helped. "During every session of the legislature there are always one or two new members who distinguish themselves," said Stratton Taylor, her friend and colleague in the legislature. "Carolyn was one of those this time. She was a star. She speaks well but chooses her issues and times carefully. She has that unusual ability to work in harmony with others, to find the common chords among all groups."

CHAPTER EIGHT

Carolyn Thompson won reelection with just over 70 percent of the vote, a convincing endorsement by the people of Norman.

What lies ahead for her? She is, of course, deeply involved in the implementation of the task force's findings, and in a range of other legislative issues. But she has not forgotten her graduate studies at the University of Oklahoma. She still plans to work toward her Ph.D. in political science and government, with an emphasis on civic literacy. "There can't be anything more important for the country," she said. She wants to probe more deeply into the reasons for the widespread ignorance and apathy of most Americans about their own government and the governmental process.

"I have lots of options and alternatives to consider," she commented as she sat in Room 304-F of the capitol toward the end of another full day. She was wearing a white lace blouse with openwork sleeves that her father had bought for her on a recent trip to Germany. Around her neck was a fine gold chain with a small medallion bearing the seal of the House of Representatives.

"I could stay on in the House and perhaps move up toward the leadership. You know they've never had a woman speaker—yet. I could return full time to higher education. I might consider either teaching or administration. I've learned a lot about both areas in recent years. Teaching appeals to me, but I know the power and responsibilities of presidents and chancellors, too. Or, I could somehow try to combine the two."

Stratton Taylor feels that her most likely course might be in the field of higher education, though he acknowledges that she has clearly demonstrated the potential to move up in the legislative leadership, should she remain in the House. Her family is unsure which course she may choose, and, naturally, her friends in teaching feel that she may well return to her first love, the classroom.

Carolyn Thompson looked out the rain-streaked windows

of the capitol toward the black superstructure of Petunia #1 and some of the other oil rigs that still dot the capitol grounds. "I have always worked very hard at whatever I do," she said. "I've always been busy and felt in control of my own life and career. I think you must do that, *make* things happen, not just sit back and *let* things happen to you. I've been fortunate to have a tremendously supportive family and good friends. Those are precious assets, no matter what course you may choose."

Index

ABC-TV Sports, 5
Aetna Life and Casualty Company, 18
Ahkeah, Sam, 65
Alda, Alan, 53–55, 57
Ambach, Gordon, 163
American Bar Association (ABA), 118–119
American Friends Committee, 133–136
American Indians
  Hopi, 61
  Navajo, *see* Navajo tribe
  Nez Percé, 80
American Indian Science and Engineering Society (AISES), 80
Arizona Public Service Company, 62, 82
Arkansas State Press, 128
Ashe, Arthur, Jr., 3–18
  birthplace, 4
  career, 3, 5, 16–17
  early jobs, 5
  early training, 4, 8–15
  education, 4–5, 6–8, 10–15, 18
  family, 4–5, 11, 15, 18
  heart attack, 5, 17
  honors and awards, 3, 11–13, 15–17
  marriage, 3
  military service, 4, 15–16
  personal traits, 3, 4, 7–10, 14
  post–retirement years, 3–8, 17–18
Ashworth, Kenneth, 163
Asian Americans
  education and, 95–96
  exodus from South Vietnam, 96
AT&T Bell Laboratories, 86, 99

Babbitt, Thelma, 133
Bardwell, Myra, 119
Barker, Jim, 147, 148
Barnett, Ross, 120
Bates, Daisy, 128, 131
Bellmon, Henry, 146
Bennett, Charlotte, 112–113
Benson, Carolyn Rowe, 18
Bilingualism, 25, 63, 69, 75, 91, 94, 97, 99
Bird Dogs (Hall), 52
Blacks
  history of, as athletes, 5–6, 17–18

INDEX

Blacks (*continued*)
  integration of public schools and, 4, 47, 92, 124
  Options for Excellence Program and, 37
  racial discrimination and, 4, 10, 14, 123–124, 127–129, 131–134, 141–142
  slavery and, 6
Bosque Redondo, 77
Bradley, Joseph P., 119
Brown v. Board of Education, 4
Bryn Mawr College, 133, 134, 139
Buhite, Russell, 157
Bull, Sheldon, 57
Bunch, Tom, 113
Bureau of Indian Affairs (BIA), 22, 63, 68–69, 75
Burrows, Jim, 54

Canyon de Chelly, 76–77
Carbone, John, 118
Carson, Kit, 76–77
Catron, Louis, 50–53
Central Catholic High School (San Antonio), 27–29
Central High School (Little Rock, Ark.), 123, 129, 131, 141–142
Charity, Ron, 4, 8–9, 12
Chatham High School (Chatham, Va.), 47–49
Cisneros, Elvira, 25–26, 36
Cisneros, George, 22–23, 25
Cisneros, George, Jr., 26, 36
Cisneros, Henry, 21–38
  early career, 23, 33–34, 35–36
  education, 23, 25–35, 26–35
  extracurricular activities, 26–27, 29, 31

  family, 21–23, 25–26, 28–30, 36
  honors and awards, 30–35
  marriage, 32–33
  as mayor, 22–25, 36–38
  personal traits, 23–26, 28, 30, 31, 33, 34, 36–37
  White House Fellowship, 33–35
Civil rights movement, 16, 17, 32, 47, 124–125, 131–134, 141–142
Codetalkers, 65
College Board National Forum, 161–163
College of William and Mary, 50, 57, 95
Columbia University, 138, 140
Connors, Jimmy, 17
Cook, David, 108, 110–111, 114, 115
Le Coq Sportif, 5
Corley, Lynette, 94–95
Cremin, Lawrence, 140
Crisis at Central High School (Huckaby), 132–133

Davis Cup, 15
  Junior, 13
Dell, Donald, 15
Dern, Bruce, 56
Desegregation
  of the armed forces, 4
  school, 4, 47, 124
Discrimination
  gender, 119
  racial, *see* Racial discrimination

Earlham College (Richmond, Ind.), 133–136
Eastland, James, 117

168

INDEX

Eight Is Enough, 54
Eisenhower, Dwight D., 124
Electricity production, 62, 82–83
Esquire, 118

Faubus, Orval E., 124
Featherston, Warren, 109
Floor, Bill, 71
Ford, Betty, 56
Ford Foundation, 35
Fraley, Pamela Wood, 7

Gadd, Gloria Baker, 105–109, 111, 112, 116–117, 119
Gender discrimination, 119
George Washington University, 23, 33
Granby High School (Norfolk, Va.), 91–96
Graves, Thomas A., Jr., 50
Green, Walter, 92, 93–94
GTE, 125, 126, 139–142
Guidance Information System (GIS), 93

Hall, Barbara, 43, 45, 46, 57
Hall, Ervis, 45, 48
Hall, Flo, 44, 48
Hall, Karen, 41–58
  birthplace, 43
  career, 41–43, 54–58
  early jobs, 54, 55
  education, 42–54
  extracurricular activities, 46, 48
  family, 43–45, 48–50, 53–55, 57
  honors and awards, 41, 46, 53, 55–56
  marriage, 57
  personal traits, 44–46, 48–51

Hamilton, Donna, 155–156
Hamner, Earl, 42, 47, 52, 55
Hard Road to Glory, A (Ashe), 3, 6, 17–18
Hart, David, 117–118
Harvard University, 23, 35
Higher Educational Opportunity Program (HEOP), 136–139
Hill Street Blues, 41, 55–56
Honn, William and Dana, 90–91
Hopi tribe, 61
Horton, Frank, 161
Huckaby, Elizabeth, 132–133
Hudlin, Richard, 11

IBM Corporation, 98, 104, 108, 114
Integration, 47, 92, 124
Iona College, 136–139, 140

Jackson, Isaiah, 7
Jackson School of Law (Mississippi College School of Law), 103, 114, 118
Japan, 135
John F. Kennedy School of Government, 35
Johnson, Robert, 9–12
Jordan, Leslie and Lorraine, 127–130
Jordan, Sybil, *see* Stevenson, Sybil Jordan
Joyce, James, 49

Kahn, Annie, 69, 75, 76
Kahn, Anthony, 61–83
  art of, 68, 79
  birthplace, 62
  career, 62–65, 82–83
  early jobs, 66, 70, 79, 81–82

169

INDEX

Kahn, Anthony, (*continued*)
  education, 62, 66, 69, 70–73, 75, 77–82
  extracurricular activities, 71–72, 74, 79–80
  family, 61, 63, 67–70, 73–76, 81, 82
  honors and awards, 66, 72, 82
  personal traits, 63, 66, 81–82
Kean, Thomas, 163
Kelleher, Bob, 15
Kennedy, Joey, 7
Kennedy, John F., 152
  assassination, 16, 29
  inauguration, 133
Kennedy, Robert, 29
  assassination, 16
Kershen, Drew, 158
King, Martin Luther, Jr., 152
  assassination, 16

Lafayette High School (Lexington, Ky.), 107–110
Larimore, James, 66, 81
Larry King Live, 38
Lieu, Thuong, 86, 99
Lieu, Winston Hong, 85–100
  career, 98–100
  early jobs, 85, 93, 94, 97–98
  education, 86, 87, 89, 90–100
  escape from South Vietnam, 87–90
  extracurricular activities, 85
  family, 86–91, 96–99
  honors and awards, 86, 92, 94, 96–97, 98
  personal traits, 86, 90, 93–95
Luong, Nhan, 87

MacDonald, Peter, 65–66, 73
McMurtrey, Martin, 27–29

Maggie Walker High School (Richmond, Va.), 4, 6–8, 12, 18
Marshall School (Richmond, Va.), 6
*M*A*S*H*, 41, 52, 53, 55
Matthews, Jesse, 124
Mexican Americans
  education and, 30, 32
  monument to, 24
  Options for Excellence Program and, 37
  racial discrimination and, 30
Miller, Frank, 149, 151
Miller, Jo Anne, 150, 156, 158
Mississippi College School of Law (Jackson School of Law), 103, 114, 118
Model Cities program, 32–33
Moonlighting, 42, 56
Morgan, J. D., 12–15
Morris, J. R., 156, 161
Moutoussamy, Jean, 3

National Geographic, 5
National League of Cities, 33
National Scholarship Service and Fund for Negro Students (NSSFNS), 133, 134
Native Americans, *see* American Indians
Navajo Coal Company, 63
Navajo Mission Academy, 70–73
Navajo tribe
  education and, 62, 63, 65, 68–69, 70–71, 77
  identity issues, 61–62, 75
  "Long Walk" of, 76–77
  reservation, 62, 64–67, 70, 73–74, 77

INDEX

size of, 83
standard of living, 64–67
traditional versus modern attitudes, 63
unemployment and, 67
Newman, Frank, 163
Newton, Corinne, 106
Newton, Suzanne, *see* Saunders, Suzanne
Norman High School (Norman, Okla.), 152–154

O'Donnell, Charles, 138
Offer, Francis, 137–139
Oil, 67, 145, 159
Okker, Tom, 16–17
Old Dominion University (Norfolk, Va.), 85, 96–99
Options for Excellence Program, 37
Osmonds, 46

Peabody Coal Company, 67
Perez, Mary Alice, 32–33
Philanthropy, corporate, 126, 139–142
Platero, Dillon, 71
Plunkett, Jim, 72
Poison Gas (Hall), 54
Portrait of the Artist as a Young Man (Joyce), 49
Powell, Marvin, 7
Power, Jim, 154
ProServ Corporation, 3, 17

Quakers, 133–136

Racial discrimination, 14
 in education, 4, 10, 30
 in the South, 123–124, 127–129, 131–134, 141–142
 in South Africa, 17
 in tennis, 8, 10, 11, 14

Remick, Lee, 56
Richardson, Elliot, 34

Saunders, Abel, and Fortenberry, 104, 120
Saunders, Hubbard T., IV, 117
Saunders, Suzanne, 103–120
 career, 103–105, 115–120
 children, 108–112, 114–117
 divorce, 115, 117
 early jobs, 103, 104, 106, 111–112, 114–115
 education, 103, 104, 107–115
 extracurricular activities, 107, 108, 112, 115
 family, 104–108
 honors and awards, 104–105, 115, 118–119
 marriages, 104, 108, 114, 115, 117
 nursery business, 110–111
 personal traits, 104–109, 111–113, 115–116
Segregation, 4, 17
 in tennis, 8, 10, 11, 14
Sexism, 119
60 Minutes, 23, 38
Slavery, 6
Smith, James, 117
Smith, Stan, 17
Smith, Viola, 153–154
South Africa, 17
Southern Methodist University, 99–100
South Vietnam, 85–88, 100
 exodus from, 96
 Vietnam War, 15, 16
Speckles, Elmo, 117
"Spencer's Mountain" (Hamner), 47
Sputnik, 7

171

INDEX

Stanford University, 62, 66, 72–73, 76, 78–82
Stark, Wayne, 31–32, 34–37
Steen, John Thomas, 36
Stevenson, John, 135–136
Stevenson, Sybil Jordan, 123–142
  career, 125–126, 136–142
  early jobs, 128, 136
  education, 123–125, 129–136, 138–140
  extracurricular activities, 130, 132
  family, 126–131
  honors and awards, 124, 125, 133–136, 140, 141
  marriage, 135–136
  personal traits, 125, 126, 138, 139
Sumner High School (St. Louis), 11–12

Taxi, 54
Taylor, Stratton, 149, 161, 163, 164
Texas A&M University, 29–32
Thompson, Carolyn, 145–165
  campaign of 1984, 157–159
  campaign of 1986, 162–164
  career, 145–150, 154, 155–165
  early jobs, 150–151
  education, 147, 150–155, 157, 159, 164
  education task force and, 160–161
  extracurricular activities, 150, 152–155
  family, 146, 147, 149, 150–152, 158
  honors and awards, 146–147, 150, 153, 157–159
  marriage, 155
  personal traits, 146–150, 155–156, 159, 160
Thompson, Richard, 155
Today show, 23
Todd, Elsie, 44, 45, 47–50, 57
Toughlove, 56
Trinh, Man, 86
Trinity University, 37
Truman, Harry, 4
Twentieth Century Fox, 41, 46

United Nations, 96
U.S. Lawn Tennis Association, 12
U.S. Military Academy (West Point), 15–16
U.S. Open Tennis Championship (Forest Hills), 16–17
U.S. Open Tennis Championship (Wimbledon), 3
University of California at Los Angeles, 4, 12–15
University of Chicago, 136
University of Kentucky, 104, 108, 109, 110
University of Oklahoma, 147, 154–157, 164
University of Richmond, 52–53
University of Texas, 23, 35
University of Virginia, 53–54
Uranium, 67

Vietnam War, 15, 16

Walker, Maggie, 6
The Waltons, 46–47, 53
Washington Post, 35
Webb, Carol, 80, 82
Weber, Jerry, 156
Wells, Linda Bradford, 81–82

INDEX

White House Fellowship, 33–35
Who's Who Among American High School Students, 46
Wilbourne, Bryant, 57
Williams, Ralph, 7
Women
  as attorneys, 104, 119
  in government, 146
  in television, 42, 55
World Book Encyclopedia, 5
World War II, 22, 65, 77, 127–128

Yeager, Chuck, 27